C000172939

Joining Jesus on His Journey

Experiencing Truth Through Imaginative Prayer

A Ten Week Retreat in Daily Life

Adrian C. Smith

PUBLISHING

This Edition Copyright © 2019 Adrian C. Smith

23 22 21 20 19   7 6 5 4 3 2 1

First published 2019 by Malcolm Down Publishing Ltd.
www.malcolmdown.co.uk

The right of Adrian C. Smith to be identified as the author of this work
has been asserted by him in accordance with the Copyright, Designs
and Patents Act 1988.

All rights reserved. No part of this publication may be reproduced,
stored in a retrieval system, or transmitted in any other form or by any
means, electronic, mechanical, photocopying, recording or otherwise,
without the prior permission of the publisher.

British Library Cataloguing in Publication Data
A catalogue record for this book is available from the British Library.

ISBN 978-1-912863-26-6

Unless otherwise indicated, Scripture quotations taken from:

New International Version (Anglicised edition)
Copyright ©1979, 1984, 2011 by Biblica (formerly International Bible
Society). Used by permission of Hodder & Stoughton Publishers,
an Hachette UK company. All rights reserved. 'NIV' is a registered
trademark of Biblica (formerly International Bible Society). UK
trademark number 1448790.

Cover Image by Nate Rayfield, Unsplash
Cover design by Esther Kotecha

Art direction by Sarah Grace

Printed in the UK

Dedication

For my grandchildren – Callum, Cole, Eden, Elliot, Jamie, Benjamin and Amelie. I love you guys. Here's something for you to remember from Grandpa, still on his journey with Jesus.

Endorsements

With a heart for God and a care and attention to detail, allied to a deep desire to journey beyond the familiar and predictable pathways of faith, the writer takes the reader on a journey of discovery. Authentic and accessible, simple yet profound, the author introduces the reader to the Ignatian Spiritual Exercises and an appreciation of other streams of spirituality. Readers will be greatly helped and encouraged to discover more about the transforming friendship that comes through knowing Christ and the adventure of faith that not only informs the mind but inspires the heart.

Roy Searle, Northumbria Community, Free Church Tutor at Cranmer Hall, Durham University, former President of the Baptist Union of Great Britain

Most good things take time. This book is no exception. You have in your hands the fruits of a man who has lived faithfully, in every sense of that word. Adrian has loved Jesus deeply, studied his word closely and received his Spirit richly for a long time. Now it is your turn! Seventy days that will wonderfully enrich your relationship with Jesus and your walk with God. Welcome on board!

Ian Galloway, Founding Pastor, City Church, Newcastle upon Tyne

In the busyness of leading a multisite church, times spent with Jesus are life giving and crucial to our spiritual heath. We can't endorse this book any more fervently, Adrian has so much to say and teach about growing in intimacy with Jesus. If this is what you desire we would encourage you to prioritize reading this book and putting all that he suggests into action.

David and Nicola Bass, Senior Pastors of Life Vineyard Church, Newcastle upon Tyne

For anyone wishing to deepen their relationship with Jesus through a retreat in daily life, this book is an ideal resource. Rooted in the writer's experience of the Ignatian Spiritual Exercises, it is clearly laid out, easy to follow and accessible to both those just setting out on their journey as well as those further along the road. It can be taken at each one's own pace and anyone can engage with it wherever they are on their spiritual journey.

Sister Sheila McNamara, Society of the Sacred Heart, Spiritual Director and Trainer in Spiritual Accompaniment

Joining Jesus on His Journey, is the fruit of a life well lived in the company and friendship of Christ. In its pages you will be stirred to walk with God, listen to His voice and re-orient your life to one of worship and wonder. In an age of multiple distractions, this book will calm your soul to delight in Jesus again. This is what we were all born for, above all other pursuits. Read this book and then practice its message.

Phil Wilthew, Senior Leader Kings Arms Church, Bedford and author of Multiplying Disciples and Developing Prophetic Culture

Adrian in this book gives us a great gift, for he shares with us his inner life with God, which has been brought new energy and life through imaginative prayer. Through sharing his experiences of meeting God afresh in scripture, he reminds us of the transformative nature of prayer, and how our imaginations can be a way of bringing us in touch with the living God, whose desire is to dwell within each and every one of us, if only we will let him in. Heartening, hopeful, vulnerable and honest, this is a book to read if you want to know yourself and God better.

The Rev'd Fr. Jonathan Lawson

Vicar of the Parish Church of St. Gabriel's, Newcastle upon Tyne

This book offers a simple and accessible introduction to Ignatian spirituality for those who are unfamiliar with the Spiritual Exercises and translates them into meditations which are easy to follow. It enables the reader to grow in their relationship with Christ, to appreciate him more, to love him more deeply. I have certainly found this to be true for me.

Paul Revill, Regional Minister (Mission), Northern Baptist Association

Acknowledgements

The contents of this book have been shaped by many people. In particular those I have led in small groups, and one-to-one prayer times, who experienced for themselves how close God is when we open our imagination to him.

Specifically I'd like to thank Paul Golightly as he led me through the Ignatian Spiritual Exercises and in our subsequent conversations. Gregory Boyd whose book Seeing is Believing placed what I was experiencing into a wider biblical context, and affirmed me. Roy Searle, Trevor Miller, Chris Collison, Catherine Askew and Judith Goodfellow of the Northumbria Community, together with Ian Galloway, David Rosser, Martyn Skinner, Paul Revill and Olusoa Idowu who gave me thoughtful advice and encouragement.

At an early and uncertain stage in the writing process Ali Hull helped me think through the concept of the book and what I wanted to achieve. At the end of the process my editor Sheila Jacobs and Malcolm Down my publisher together with Sarah Grace helped shape that concept into what you see today.

I'd also like to give special thanks to my wife, Nicky, for her patience with me as I grappled with the challenges of attempting to be a first-time author.

Contents

Foreword

———•———

I'm waiting on the slipway ready to board the first ferry of the day from the Island of Mull to Iona on the west coast of Scotland. A grey sky is accompanied by a hint of the rain that is to come later in the morning. I'm glad I put on an extra layer. The ferry comes into sight from the Bull Hole, its overnight mooring. There are just a few of us making this ten-minute crossing. With a couple of friends I'm heading to the abbey for the morning service and then a day spent on the island, walking, sitting, praying, writing and in conversation.

Back home a couple of weeks later I re-engage with that experience, only this time I imagine Jesus with me on the slipway, boarding the ferry together. Then there's time for some conversation standing on the passenger deck looking over the sea as we cross towards the small island. Just ten minutes with Jesus to talk about the day ahead, the places I will visit and the people I will see. On this journey the island represents my coming day. I'm entering my day with Jesus, wanting to be part of what he is doing today, and to see him at work in what I will be doing. Standing next to him I can sense that he is full of life and energy; it's good to be here with him.

Evening, and boarding the last ferry we meet again on the pier and then walk down the slipway to have our tickets checked. We talk about the day, its challenges and achievements. I thank him for being with me as I walked the island, experienced a soaking and then the warmth of the chapel in Bishop's House. I talk to him about a friend with terminal cancer. He challenges and affirms me; we look forward to meeting again on the slipway tomorrow.

Just ten minutes in Jesus' presence as I make the crossing into each new day and then again on the journey home.

Introduction

———•———

Encountering Jesus is to experience truth

The truth is that God loves each one of us deeply, wonderfully and unconditionally. That's why Jesus came and lived amongst us, 'full of grace and truth', as John so beautifully puts it in the opening verses of his Gospel (John 1:14).

Truth is something we come to know in many different ways, by hearing, seeing, sensing and lived experience. Hearing that God loves me gives me the desire to experience that truth. Reading in John's Gospel chapter 15 that Jesus calls me his friend makes me want to live in that truth as well.

When we encounter Jesus, truth bursts into life. We move from the realm of ideas and concepts to the reality that truth is found in a person. And what a person, someone who already knows us better than we know ourselves and is committed to drawing us ever more closely into his friendship.

What better way to grow in Jesus' love and friendship than to join him on his life journey here on earth as recorded in the Gospels? To enter and take part in the story in ways that connect you to him both then and now. To be open to the Holy Spirit as you encounter Jesus, and then see where he takes you.

This short book takes you on a ten-week journey into experiencing Jesus through Imaginative Prayer. A journey that I hope will help you to experience first-hand the truth that, in Jesus, God loves you more than you can ever comprehend. He really does!

Just before we walk down the slipway to meet Jesus and begin the journey, let me introduce myself and then in the following two short chapters explain a few things.

My journey

I'm writing this at the home of my youngest daughter in Cape Town, on an unusually wet day. Visiting with my wife, Nicky, and catching up with our three South African grandchildren is a highlight of our year. At home in the UK we have another two daughters and four more grandchildren. You will have guessed by now that I'm no spring chicken. My aim as I write is to see this book published before my 75th birthday at the end of 2019.

Before retiring I worked as a town planner in Newcastle upon Tyne (in the north-east of England), rounding off my career facilitating the development of renewable energy projects. Often I felt a lack of boundaries between my 'secular' day job and my Christian faith. The two could flow easily together, the one informing and strengthening the other.

My faith journey has been enriched by many different sources and streams. My first remembered 'spiritual' experience came before I was ten; it was simple but still memorable, the sense of presence in my room. Not something I could understand, but conveying to me that there was more – my desire for God was born. It took shape as I read the New Testament and then later with my parents began attending an Anglican church rooted in the Catholic tradition.

The years that followed as I moved, studied and married took me through a variety of expressions of Church – the Brethren, Free Evangelical, Baptist, evangelical Anglican, reformed, and then charismatic/evangelical where I have largely (but not entirely) settled.

I am stirred to present Jesus to others, and that's included preaching and praying for healing out on the street. For many years I used to lead worship and still love being lost in the presence of God as He flows through a meeting.

I'm a long-time member of City Church in Newcastle upon Tyne (part of the New Frontiers family), where I led our trustees. I still help to lead our charity, Action Foundation, which provides housing and language training for asylum seekers and refugees.

Another important strand in my journey has been as a companion member of the Northumbria Community. The Community has taught me so much about waiting in God's presence, experiencing him in silence, taking and then leading retreats.

'Not entirely settled' is probably the best description of my ongoing state of mind, content where I am, but knowing and then discovering that there is more. In spite of all my wanderings, my belief remains orthodox and I'm happy with the Evangelical Alliance's Basis of Faith. I see the Father as my creator, Jesus as my redeemer and the Spirit as the one who gives me life and insight. My desire for more of God has taken me to some interesting places over the last five years, and that's why I'm writing.

You will learn more about my recent journey as you progress through this book. It included a near-fatal heart attack (fortunately not an essential for spiritual growth), which gave me a fresh perspective on my life and how closely God is engaged with me. I trained to become a Spiritual Director and now accompany (I prefer that word) a number of people, some of whom I will introduce to you. I've included a short section on Spiritual Direction in the Appendix.

The training I received was based in part on the insights of Ignatius of Loyola, and once completed I decided to undertake the Ignatian Spiritual Exercises. I'll tell you more about that, but in brief I would say that experience changed my relationship with Jesus. He used the Exercises to draw me closer into his friendship, and the way in which that happened is central to the content of this ten-week retreat.

Experiencing truth through Imaginative Prayer

Over the years I have encountered God in many different ways and settings, as my brief history indicates. If encountering Jesus is to experience truth, how does this happen? There are so many possible answers to that question, and many excellent books that provide insight and approaches. I'm not the right person to provide a comprehensive overview, I want to focus here on ways of encountering Jesus that have come alive for me and the people I 'accompany'. Some of this may appear to be new, but in fact I'm going to describe approaches to prayer that are centuries old, and which can be observed in the Scriptures.

First let me give you three recent examples – from Miye, Carol and Phil.

Miye is a member of City Church and kindly agreed to work through the material in this book when it was still at a draft stage. I'm grateful to her and others who gave me feedback which helped to shape what you are now reading. This book is set out as a 'Ten Week Retreat in Daily Life' and each 'week' includes a day of 'resting prayer'. (An explanation as to how this works follows shortly.) During the Week 3 time of resting prayer, Miye recorded the following encounter with Jesus in her journal:

I'm on Bamburgh beach with Jesus. It's a warm sunny day. He says, 'Let's go for a walk along the beach.' Suddenly I'm a child with a kite running along the beach, sometimes ahead of Jesus and other times with Jesus holding my hand. Sometimes he carries me on his shoulder. I am giggling and laughing for no apparent reason. He asks if I'm enjoying the time with him. I say, 'Yes, it's so much fun.' He says, 'I'm delighted in spending time with you. In fact, I'm always with you wherever you are. If you want to feel my presence just close your eyes and be still. You are my delight. You are my beloved child. You don't need to do anything. Just be my daughter. You already are!'

What a wonderful encounter with Jesus! Miye was experiencing things, in her imagination, she knew to be true – that she is God's beloved child; that she doesn't have to do anything to achieve that, she already is. She already knew everything that Jesus said to her that day; she could check his words against Scripture if she had needed to. But the encounter added an extra dimension to what she knew. Jesus spoke those words directly to her, he held her, carried her, they walked hand in hand. She experienced truth, albeit in her imagination, within the image of childlike faith.

Carol is also happy for me to share her story. I've been accompanying Carol on her journey with Jesus for over two years. We meet every two to three months for conversation and prayer in the Methodist church Carol is part of. During our early conversations Carol was struggling with her many commitments, feeling that she needed to make changes and drop some of her activities. But how to do that, and what about the sense of letting others down? There were some relationship issues as well which were possibly holding her back.

At one of our meetings I decided to use the story of Jesus healing the man with the withered hand recorded in Mark 3 as the starting point for our prayer time. I invited Carol to imagine herself in the synagogue witnessing the hostility focused on Jesus and then see him heal the man's hand. I then suggested that she reach out her hand to Jesus and see what he would do. I gave her five or so minutes in silence and then she told me about her encounter.

In her imagination she stretched out her hand towards Jesus and then saw him stretch out his hand towards her. To her surprise his hand went into her heart and he began to remove small stones, one at a time, that turned to dust in his fingers as they came out. No words were spoken but this was a transactional moment, Jesus was healing something in Carol's life. As she described this to me, she referred to an outstanding issue with someone and said that she no longer needed to take any action, it had been dealt with.

At our next meeting I asked if she had needed to follow anything up with the person in question and again Carol confirmed that no action was necessary and she had been able to move forward.

Phil is also a member of City Church and this encounter happened as he took part in one of our day retreats. The lead in was meeting Jesus in the temple.

I imagined myself approaching Jesus, but there were lots of people crowding around him. Jesus looked through the crowd, saw me, and walked towards me. He said he'd been looking out for me, and asked if I'd like to walk with him. I said yes, but that I hadn't been there before so I didn't know where we could go. He said, 'We can walk through the temple if you like, but I want to show you that you don't need to come here to meet with me.'

Suddenly Jesus and I were sitting on the floor in my living room, helping my children to do a jigsaw. Then, we were in the fruit and veg aisle at the supermarket, and Jesus helped me get the fruit and veg for my shopping. Then, Jesus was in the passenger seat of my car as I drove around at work (I'm a driving instructor), and when we arrived to meet a learner for my next lesson, Jesus got out, and got in the back so I could have the passenger seat for the lesson, and off we all went.

Then we were back in the temple, and Jesus said, 'Don't forget that I'm with you every minute of the day. I'm with you in the places I've just shown you, and everywhere else. Even in the mundane jobs like picking your fruit and veg!

You don't need to make a special effort on special occasions like the high priest in the Holy of Holies; we can just spend time together whenever and wherever you like, whatever you might be doing.

Three very different encounters, one initiated by Jesus during a time of personal quiet prayer, the second taking place in the context of Spiritual Direction, using an event during Jesus' own journey here on earth as the starting point. The third was experienced in a group setting, with a common starting point that led off in many different directions. In each case, and the many others I have not included, the experience was tailor-made for the individual concerned. It showed them important truths about their relationship with God, and in particular how Jesus, by his Spirit, is closely engaged in the detail of their lives.

In the next two chapters I want to explore what can help you experience Jesus in the ways I've been describing. I'm also going to take a look at some of the questions this way of praying raises, possible pitfalls and ways of doing this well.

Then I hope you will be ready to embark on the ten-week journey, experiencing more of Jesus and being drawn into his friendship – walking down the 'slipway' with Jesus as this particular journey begins.

1. Joining Jesus on His Journey: How Does That Work?

In this chapter I'm going to unpack what I understand about Imaginative Prayer and Conversational Journaling. I'll also introduce the Ignatian Spiritual Exercises. These are ways of encountering God that I, and many before me, have found bring life into the relationship. I'm sharing what I've experienced so far but I'm on a learning curve, even at my age, so I may not be able to answer all the questions you might have. And I still have some of my own.

What follows is pitched at an introductory level, adequate I hope to help you engage with this Ten Week Retreat. I'm not going to provide an in-depth explanation of these ways of praying. And fortunately, that's not necessary; others have done that, and inspired me in the process. I'll signpost authors and books that I've found to be particularly helpful.

I also want to emphasise that the ways of encountering God I'm focusing on here do not replace others that are equally valuable. There may be a risk that what I've written could be read narrowly, with the implication that this is 'the' way to do it. Far from it; as my brief history indicates I find great benefit in a wide range of spiritual disciplines and approaches. I love the power of worshipping in the Spirit in a large congregation, reflective liturgy in a monastic setting, intercession in personal and church contexts, and reflecting on Scripture. It's important to maintain a balance, and not to become focused on a few ways of approaching God. At the same time, I would say it's equally important to pursue what is life-giving, and that may vary as you pass through different seasons.

For example, this morning in my prayer time I received encouragement from Psalm 90:17. Writing can be a hard and at times discouraging process, so I was happy to join the psalmist in praying: 'May the favour of the Lord our God rest on us; establish the work of our hands for us – yes, establish the work of our hands.' I'll let you judge how far that particular prayer has been answered! I also discovered that the Northumbria Community Prayer Guide for that particular morning was focused on those who are seeking to write. I was duly encouraged and felt that God was on my case.

This book does not provide a comprehensive overview on ways of praying. Rather my hope is that it will encourage you to explore what may be new ways of prayer that can comfortably fit within a balanced approach to seeking and worshipping God. That's been my experience. What follows has added to my prayer life and enriched it, particularly when praying for others, including those with terminal illnesses. (I've included an example drawn from the experience of my friend John at the close of this book.)

The starting point is that God, Father, Son and Spirit, loves to be with us, speak to us and draw us into his friendship and confidence. We can see that demonstrated in the relationship between Jesus and his first disciples. The three examples I've included above do the same and you may have your own stories of God's goodness and love. That desire for relationship is extended to those who do not yet know him.

The connecting point is desire – our desire for God. In her book *Sister Wendy on Prayer*, Wendy Beckett says that 'The essential act of prayer is to stand unprotected before God'. She asks 'What will God do?', and answers 'He will take possession of us. That He should do this is the whole purpose of life.'[1] It sounds scary but I think I have had a few moments when this has happened to me. Do I really want to be possessed by God, or do I just wish I had such a desire? Desire is the key; what do I really want, to be close but not too close, or fully embraced by God who loves me eternally? I definitely want more, whatever that means. If Sister Wendy is right, that's enough for God to begin graciously drawing me closer to himself. The same is true for those yet to commence a journey of faith.

God's love is the starting point and our desire for him is part of making the connection. Let's move forward now and look at two specific approaches that can help to make that connection and which will lead us into the Ten Week Retreat.

Imaginative Prayer

In Ephesians 2:6-7, Paul says:

---

1. Sister Wendy Beckett, *Sister Wendy on Prayer* (London: Bloomsbury Continuum, 2008). (See Section 1 The Practice of Prayer Your Unique Prayer).

And God raised us up with Christ and seated us with him
in the heavenly realms in Christ Jesus, in order that in the
coming ages he might show the incomparable riches of his
grace, expressed in his kindness to us in Christ Jesus.

It seems that it's possible to be in two places at once! Here, wherever
you happen to be on planet Earth, and with Christ where he is.
Part of God's purpose in making this possible is to show us things
– in particular 'the incomparable riches of his grace'. There is
nothing that can outmatch the grace, love and goodness of God.
He wants us to be with Jesus so that we can see and experience
this for ourselves.

I want to suggest that Imaginative Prayer is one way by which we
can enter into what Paul is seeking to describe in the verses above.
Paul is describing a really big concept, hard to fully understand,
but relatively easy to experience. God wants us to be with Jesus
so that he can show us who he is and how much he loves us. Let's
take a closer look.

Imaginative Prayer is a way of engaging with the Gospel stories
not just as an outside observer 2,000 years after the event, but
more as a participant. My first exposure to this kind of prayer
came in a small group where the leader took us into the familiar
story of the healing of Bartimaeus, recorded in Mark 10 (we will
return to that story later). As she read the passage and described
the setting, I entered the story in my imagination as a bystander. I
edged my way into the crowd for a better look at what was going
on, getting as close to Jesus as I could. I felt the excitement as

Bartimaeus was healed and could see. Then as the crowd shouted in delight Jesus moved to one side, towards me, and asked me the question he had just put to Bartimaeus: 'What do you want me to do for you?' What a question to be asked by Jesus!

That was the start; tentative and uncertain to begin with, but one which opened up a fresh way of meeting Jesus. Over the last five or so years I've found that this way of praying changes and develops with practice. I've led small groups where I've seen many people, uncertain and sceptical, finding to their surprise a living connection with Jesus as they engage in this way of praying. It could be someone seeking to know Jesus for the very first time, or a veteran such as myself.

It's certainly not a new approach to prayer but one that has been practised for centuries. In the past it has gone by the title Cataphatic Prayer (sometimes spelt with a K). It can also be referred to as 'Ignatian Prayer' because its use is encouraged when undertaking the Ignatian Spiritual Exercises. It's true that Ignatius of Loyola popularised this way of praying back in the sixteenth century, but it predates him.

There are so many instances in Scripture where God communicates with people using images as well as words to get a point across. A well-known example would be that of the ladder Jacob saw in a dream linking heaven and earth (Genesis 28:10-22). That big picture image provided the backdrop for God's specific words to Jacob about his destiny and that of his descendants. It was a transactional moment, Jacob experienced the unanticipated presence of God, and it changed the course of his life. It's interesting to note that he sought to capture what had happened by setting up and naming a marker to remind future generations about his encounter with God. Maybe that was his way of 'journaling'.

Another example would be in Acts 10 which provides a detailed account of Peter being shown a large sheet containing all kinds of animals, and being instructed by God as to what he should do. In Revelation 1:10 John begins his account of what he saw as he waited on God 'in the Spirit'.

This is familiar ground; Scripture is full of God communicating with people in a wide variety of ways. Sometimes they were actively seeking him; sometimes the exchange came in a vision or dream. There were times when God spoke with an audible voice and more than one person got to hear the message – for example, the voice from heaven at Jesus' baptism (Matthew 3:16-17), and at the transfiguration (Matthew 17:1-5). But in most instances the communication seems to have taken place one-to-one, at a private level. For example, Daniel refers to visions he received that 'passed through his mind', implying that they were subjective, personal experiences (Daniel 7:1,15).

The person at the receiving end experienced God communicating with them in their mind, often in ways that touched their emotions. We can say God uses our imagination as a vehicle for communication.

In his book *Seeing is Believing*, Gregory Boyd makes the point that Western societies often identify the imagination with make-believe, and thereby question or deny the authenticity of experiences recorded throughout Scripture. In contrast people in biblical times generally knew that the imagination was a means by which God did communicate, when they were awake or asleep.[2] I've observed what Boyd is referring to in conversation with Iranian friends who have no problem with the idea of God communicating in these ways; it seems to be generally accepted in their culture.

Is experiencing God in your imagination something that happens spontaneously at God's initiative, or is it something to be cultivated that can happily sit alongside other spiritual disciplines? Certainly there are times when the initiative rests entirely with God, and dreams would seem to fit within that category. But Paul seems to suggest that this is also something we can actively engage in as we seek to grow in our relationship with Jesus.

> Now the Lord is the Spirit, and where the Spirit of the Lord is, there is freedom. And we all, who with unveiled faces contemplate the Lord's glory, are being transformed into his image with ever-increasing glory, which comes from the Lord, who is the Spirit. (2 Corinthians 3:17-18)

Looking at the Lord's glory, however you do that, changes you – how could it be otherwise! The starting point can be considering truths set out in Scripture, seeing the hand of God in creation, experiencing him in your imagination, or preferably in every way possible!

As you navigate this Ten Week Retreat you will be in a position to test for yourself whether actively using your imagination to engage with Jesus has the transforming effect that Paul speaks about. Paul makes the point that this is a progressive process, we

---

2. Gregory A. Boyd, *Seeing is Believing: Experience Jesus through Imaginative Prayer* (Grand Rapids, MI: Baker Books, 2004). (See page 86).

are being transformed. In 1 Corinthians 13:12 he also says that what we do see is like a poor reflection in a mirror. It's not 20/20 vision. However, even though our experience may be partial, as Paul says, it contributes towards a transforming process. That has been my experience, a gradual and still incomplete transformation of my relationship with Jesus. Often initiated by him in ways I didn't see coming.

This way of praying doesn't replace other ways we find helpful; it adds to and enriches them. For more background, explanation and detail on Imaginative Prayer I recommend that you read Gregory Boyd's book, *Seeing is Believing*.

Engaging in any kind of prayer is a bit like dancing; you can read about it, hear from and watch others, get the ideas and concepts into your head, but the only way to really learn is to get out onto the floor and try out it for yourself. How to do this will vary for each individual as you work your way through the 'Ten Weeks'.

Conversational Journaling

Imaginative Prayer is one way of connecting to Jesus, which can be rich in images and words. It is very helpful to complement this way of praying with journaling in order not to lose what you have experienced, or heard. Like prayer, journaling can take many forms. Simply noting what you are thinking and experiencing captures the moment and allows you to reflect later.

I've found that images and storylines experienced during Imaginative Prayer can build and develop over time and journaling is one way of facilitating this process. Sometimes God gives a big picture, like the one he gave to Jacob, which stretches the present way into the future. I'm thinking here of someone I pray with occasionally who was recently bereaved. She was led by Jesus though the image of a dark wood that spoke clearly of her circumstances at the time, to a place where she could reconnect with her journey and where there was a sense of a new day about to begin. Journaling that kind of experience enables you to see how far you have moved forward and what is still to come.

I've kept a journal on and off over the years in which I record insights and times when I have sensed God speaking to me in a particular way. Times of crisis and questioning, plus significant dreams, have an important place in that record of life. Writing helps to focus my attention – what really was going on, what did I hear or experience? I want to be clear before I commit to paper, even if I am the only reader. Initially my journal was mostly thoughts and reflections; over time it has become the record of an ongoing conversation.

I discovered the practice of Conversational Journaling in a book by Helen Cepero, *Journaling as a Spiritual Practice: Encountering God through Attentive Writing.*[3] I remember taking my first tentative steps, writing my name on a fresh sheet of paper and the things I was thinking about that morning. Then leaving some space on the page and writing 'God' on a new line, I stopped to listen for that gentle whisper. I was not disappointed, but I had lots of questions and some uncertainty.

As I began to practise Conversational Journaling at times my surroundings provided the trigger for a conversation with God, but generally the starting point was a passage or verse in Scripture.

---

3. Helen Cepero, *Journaling as a Spiritual Practice: Encountering God through Attentive Writing* (Downers Grove, IL: InterVarsity Press, 2008). (See Chapter 10 Talking Back – Dialogue Journaling).

Sometimes what I heard from him and wrote about went off at a tangent from my starting point. Gradually I have become more open to being led by the Holy Spirit.

Let me give you a couple of examples. Early in my journey through the Ignatian Spiritual Exercises I considered the image of a ploughed field as a way of preparing myself for the future. I thought about some fields I had just seen being ploughed when out cycling, and the process of breaking up compacted soil releasing nutrients buried deep down. The conversation went something like this:

Adrian: I wonder if I am a field being prepared for a new season; am I in for some deep or shallow ploughing?

Here is what I sensed and wrote down as a reply:

Jesus: … you are a field I have been working on and preparing for many years. I have already seen a number of harvests and the field has changed under my care. Now I am ploughing and preparing you again for more. I have specific new crops for you to yield and my attention right now is to prepare you for them. The soil is good but there are places that need to be broken up and made ready. Know that I am doing this.

That was a particularly encouraging conversation in 2014. Looking back, I can now see how the reply I received has worked out over the intervening years. There has been some deep ploughing going on, and certainly some new and unexpected 'crops', including the text I am currently writing.

More recently, from my journal in December 2018, I was reading through John's first letter, 1 John 5:21 – 'Dear children, keep yourselves from idols' – the conversation went like this:

Adrian: A hard question, what are my idols? My first thought is myself, not that I worship myself but I orientate things, resources, time around myself … Help me keep my focus on you and not the things I am seeking to do for you. If my relationship with you is central then the idols will be shown up for what they are.

Here is what I sensed and wrote down as a reply:

Jesus: Allow me to hold you, for that is the starting and finishing point. Rest in me and things will unfold. You will see your idols for what they are – worthless idols compared with the joy you will experience in knowing me, being in me. Let's travel today in each other's company, you have much to do.

Again this was very encouraging. Jesus knows about the things I struggle with, I hold no surprises for him. He invites me to rest in him and travel with him throughout my day.

I came across Imaginative Prayer and Conversational Journaling separately, but now after a few years of practice I can see how well they work together. When leading people in Imaginative Prayer in a small group setting, I might ask them to enter a scene from the Gospels, for example, the healing of Bartimaeus in Mark 10. Then as they engage with Jesus in the context of that story, I invite them to hear Jesus' question addressed to themselves: 'What do you want me to do for you?' I suggest that they write their reply and then under Jesus' name add anything they sense him saying to them. It can be a single exchange, or a lengthy backwards and forwards conversation. Sometimes Jesus takes people out of the story they started in to somewhere else, in which case the written conversation tracks what is happening.

Using a journal to complement Imaginative Prayer, when engaging in conversation, can also be a helpful safeguard. It provides a record that can be used to talk through what you are experiencing with someone you trust.

The Ignatian Spiritual Exercises

Having experienced more of the presence of Jesus through Imaginative Prayer and Conversational Journaling, I decided to embark on what turned out to be a nine-month journey with him. Starting with the visit of the angel to Mary and concluding at his Ascension, I followed a well-travelled route provided by the Ignatian Spiritual Exercises. The Exercises are not part of my church tradition; they were well off my radar. I approached them with some uncertainty but was attracted by the prospect of joining Jesus on a daily basis in the Gospel story and seeing where that would take me.

I'm introducing the Ignatian Spiritual Exercises because the journal I kept during my nine-month journey has provided the source material for most of what follows in this Ten Week Retreat.

The Ignatian Spiritual Exercises require some discipline – for me a significant commitment of time, about forty minutes to an hour each day, six days a week, plus regular fortnightly meetings with Paul Golightly at St Antony's Priory in Durham who directed me over that nine-month period.

The Exercises were devised by Ignatius of Loyola who was born in the Basque region of Northern Spain in 1491. Ignatius is perhaps best known for founding the Jesuit Order within the Catholic Church. The Exercises were developed over a lengthy period as a way of helping people to experience God, enjoy greater freedom and live a purposeful life.

They are meant to be experienced, not just read about. I often started my prayer time with the briefest of instruction in the notes I was using, thinking, 'This is going nowhere special,' only to be amazed as I landed at the other end. God used the Ignatian Spiritual Exercises to reach someone coming from an evangelical/charismatic background in ways I had never experienced before.

The notes I followed were prepared by Sister Elizabeth Hallett, and are entitled, *The Spiritual Exercises of St Ignatius in Daily Life for 21st Century Ecumenical Men and Women*. Sister Hallett was a member of La Retraite Convent in London, and her notes were made available to St Antony's Priory but never published.

My retreat director Paul Golightly explained that Ignatius recommends that in undertaking the Exercises you imagine speaking to God as one friend speaks to another. Ignatius called this a 'colloquy'. I had already been practising this approach through Conversational Journaling. It seemed natural to continue this and capture both my own reactions and what I was receiving from God. Somehow this way of journaling helped me become more attentive and focused.

That nine-month experience of meeting Jesus on his journey recorded in the Gospel stories began to change my relationship with him. Conversation and friendship are inseparable. Growing in friendship with Jesus is about speaking, listening, carefully noting and reflecting. Over time you begin to see a train of thought, things that come up regularly, challenges, affirmation and encouragement. The conversation widens and begins to cover different topics; sometimes he breaks in and redirects the whole flow of what is being said.

This way of entering the Gospel story engaged both my mind and emotions. I tend to be analytical when I'm reading the Bible. Entering the story was different; I felt apprehensive as Jesus entered Jerusalem on a donkey and horror at his crucifixion. But I needed to be there, with my friend, watching and waiting. Friendship held me in the story.

The majority of people I know are unlikely to undertake the Ignatian Spiritual Exercises. My hope is that some of what I have learned and experienced, together with the journey outlined in this Ten Week Retreat, will draw you further into Jesus' friendship.

Hearing God speak

You've come with me this far, but I'm wondering if you find the idea of meeting God in your imagination or having a written conversation with Jesus all a bit strange, and maybe risky. How do I know this is God and not just me? It is certainly possible that imagination can mislead. There is a need for both caution and safeguarding, and I'd like to consider those issues now.

Scripture has plenty of warnings about the danger of false prophecy. For example, Ezekiel 13:2-3,17:

… Say to those who prophesy out of their own imagination: Hear the word of the LORD!' This is what the Sovereign LORD says: woe to the foolish prophets who follow their own spirit and have seen nothing!' … 'Now son of man, set your face against the daughters of your people who prophesy out of their own imagination.'

It's possible to be misled, or simply just get it wrong. That in itself is not a reason for sidelining prophetic gifting or seeking to encounter God in the ways I've just been describing. It is, however, a reason to be cautious and apply some tests.

In his book *Hearing God: Developing a Conversational Relationship with God*, Dallas Willard addresses the question – is this really God or just me? Willard draws together his thoughts as follows:

In summary, then, what we discern when we learn to recognize God's voice in our heart is a certain *weight or force*, a certain *spirit* and certain *content* in the thoughts that come in God's communications to us. These three things in combination mark the voice of God. To those well experienced in the Way of Christ, these give great confidence and great accuracy in living day-to-day as the friends of Christ and as colaborers with God in his kingdom.[4]

Willard's suggestions here are helpful, but seem a bit subjective. Essentially he is saying that over time we can learn to distinguish

---

4. Dallas Willard, *Hearing God: Developing a Conversational Relationship with God* (Downers Grove IL: InterVarsity Press, 2012). (See page 235).

God's voice from others. I agree, but there are plenty of times when I'm still not exactly sure. And maybe that's a good place to be. If I found myself being sure about everything I was hearing or seeing, the one thing I'd know for certain was that something was wrong. It's good to be in a place where you can apply a degree of healthy scepticism.

Some tests you can apply

I'd like to suggest three tests that can be used which will allow us to hear more from God while staying in a safe place. They are the tests of Scripture, advice and time:

Scripture provides the first benchmark against which you can test whatever you think God is showing you. So, taking the example of Miye's experience of being with Jesus on the beach and the things he said to her, there was nothing in that exchange that as far as I can see contradicts Scripture. The words she heard from Jesus were personalised expressions of truth that can be found in many passages of the Bible. So, firstly, test what you are hearing and experiencing against Scripture and if you are still not certain, move on to the next tests.

Advice is the second test. If you are not sure about something then talk to someone whose opinion you respect and trust. I remember clearly a dream I had about fifteen years ago which showed me that my career needed a radical change of direction. It came at a moment when I was being offered a significant and financially rewarding piece of work. I asked for time and consulted two people, my wife, Nicky, and Ian, our pastor. I let the message of the dream and the advice I had been given settle and then decided against that particular contract. Advice is just that, you still have to draw your own conclusions, but it can be a very helpful safeguard.

Time is the third test. The decision I took following the work-related dream could still have been the wrong one. However, looking back I now see how this unexpected and unasked for warning redirected my journey in ways I now know have been so much better than the track I was following. In this particular case I was able to resolve the issue, and the test of time confirmed that I came to the right conclusion. There are other occasions when uncertainty remains, and then it is right to hold back and give yourself as much time as you need to make sure.

These three tests apply in many situations where we are seeking to discern God's will and leading. They should be applied fully as we encounter him in Imaginative Prayer and Conversational Journaling.

Martyn Skinner, hospital chaplain and friend suggests that over time we can move forward from the 'either/or' question (is this me or is it God), towards a 'both/and' way of hearing. In other words, hearing becomes more about God and us in union; it's a conversation where ideas and thoughts from each party blend together. Can you think of times when something new has come out of the to and fro of conversation with a friend? It can be hard to disentangle who exactly said what and where that good idea first came from.

Over the time I've been journaling in this way I've learned to step aside from the 'inner critic', always write down what I think I'm hearing, and then look more critically later.

New Age parallels?

One further area of possible concern needs to be mentioned. Some Christians have reservations about Imaginative Prayer as they see apparently similar practices being used within the New Age Movement. Gregory Boyd in his book *Seeing is Believing* addresses this issue comprehensively. He points out that the practice of imaginatively beholding the Lord is as old as Christianity itself. I've made the same point drawing from Ephesians 2:6-7. It would be difficult to do justice to Boyd's treatment of this topic in summary and I suggest that you look at his work if this is something that particularly concerns you.

The starting point

In rounding off this section on tests that you can apply to what you hear or experience, let's go back to the starting point which is a desire to hear from God. We are seeking to encounter Jesus, and be led by the Holy Spirit. And in that context my faith is based on Jesus' words in Luke 11:11-13:

> Which of you fathers, if your son asks you for a fish, will give him a snake instead? Or if he asks for an egg, will give him a scorpion? If you then, though you are evil, know how to give good gifts to your children, how much more will your Father in heaven give the Holy Spirit to those who ask him!

This is the place to start from, but it's still important to test things properly, including seeking advice.

2. How to Navigate the Ten Weeks

———·———

Having described the approaches to prayer that I hope will help you to engage with God over this Ten Week Retreat, I want to outline some practical aspects of this journey.

What is a 'Retreat in Daily Life'?

A prayer retreat is an opportunity to spend more time than is usually possible in God's presence. In essence it's about intentionally creating space and allowing time to be with him and see your friendship grow. The key to gaining the benefit of taking a regular retreat is to find a pattern that works for you at this stage of your life.

Retreat centres are a great resource and many offer themed programmes as well as silence and one-to-one spiritual accompaniment. However, for many people, including a residential retreat into their diary is always going to be difficult, if not impossible.

It's important to think creatively about what is realistic for you, rather than focusing on an impossible ideal. How could you create more space to be with God, at home, in nature, alone, with others? What is possible perhaps once a year, monthly, weekly?

Can you make a plan that helps you build into your diary some special times when your focus will be on growing your friendship with Jesus? And in those times practise some Imaginative Prayer and Conversational Journaling? You can use a retreat, however short or long, to review your journal and see what God has been saying over time.

A 'Retreat in Daily Life' is different again. Here the idea is to capture some of the benefits of taking a prayer retreat in the midst of normal everyday life. This book has been designed to help and resource you in taking such a 'retreat'.

Before you start on this journey, think about what is realistic and sustainable for you.

Some organisation and discipline are required. How much time can you set aside in your daily schedule, and at what time of the day? Is there a particular place you will use during your prayer time – a certain room or chair?

As explained below, the material in this book is set out over ten weeks. It could equally be described as a sequence of ten stages, or steps. It really is up to you how much time you spend on each on each 'week' and each 'day'. If the content of a particular 'day' resonates strongly with you and you need further time to follow through, then do just that. Take all the time you need. As you enter into this material, let the Holy Spirit set the pace and move on when it feels right to do so.

Take your time

Friendship and the deepening of any relationship take time. Practising Imaginative Prayer and Conversational Journaling can help you encounter Jesus and through him 'experience truth' on an occasional basis, but I'm hoping that like me you want more than this. Engaging in a ten-week journey will allow that experience to build. As that happens it will begin to change you and the way you relate to Jesus. We meet him in the Gospel story and then he shows us things he wants us to see in our daily life with him.

Imaginative Prayer and Conversational Journaling seem to come easily to some people. For others this is learned behaviour that takes time to grow into. Do that, give this time; my experience suggests that you will reap a great reward.

Spiritual Companionship

Some journeys work best when travelled in company. We see that in Jesus' own life. We are called to be disciples and to travel together with him and our companions. In my brief introduction I referred to being trained in Spiritual Direction. It's rather a misleading term as the purpose is not to direct others by telling them what to do, but rather help them become more aware for themselves of what God is doing in their lives. It's primarily about listening to the other person, listening to God at the same time and then reflecting back.

Spiritual Direction is all about walking and sharing the journey together, sometimes over many years. It's not primarily about crisis management, or problem solving, but sharing life as it unfolds in the company of Jesus. It shares some common features with counselling and pastoral care, but it is different, as I hope this brief description demonstrates.

It's not essential, but you might find it helpful to share your journey alongside someone else through this Ten Week Retreat. Spiritual companions can be hard to find, but it's worth making the search. Look for someone you can trust to talk to about your experiences. A companion is there for encouragement and also as a safeguard if you are uncertain about what you are experiencing. As suggested above, it's very important to seek advice if you are unsure about what you think God is saying to you.

It may help to navigate the Ten Weeks alongside others who are doing the same thing. Feedback and discussion in a one-to-one or group context can be very helpful. As a way of testing the content of this book, I asked a number of people to engage in the Retreat and then meet to discuss. I took part in discussions with this group and saw how each member was able to encourage the other, sharing how the same material had led them in both similar and different directions.

If you are already part of a small group, maybe this is something you could do together. You would not need to commit to a particular timescale, but see how the Holy Spirit leads you.

How this book is structured

The material in this book is designed specifically to facilitate a 'Retreat in Daily Life'.

Each of the Ten Weeks is structured in the same way:
The scope of the week is introduced briefly
Days 1-4: Each day has its own meditation as a starting point

Day 5: Repetition – this is an opportunity to look back over the previous four days and spend more time on what seems most significant

Day 6: Resting prayer – an opportunity to spend time in the presence of Jesus, not with any agenda other than to enjoy him and see where that takes you

Day 7: A day off to do something different

The Week's headings are as follows:

Week 1: Preparing for Your Journey

Week 2: Preparing for Jesus' Journey

Week 3: Out of Security and into Vulnerability

Week 4: Engaging in what Jesus is Doing, Then and Now

Week 5: Walking Closely Together

In Week 6 a different approach is taken using themes drawn from the preceding weeks:

Week 6: Themes

   Image and reality

   Inner freedom

   A refuge for others

   An open door

Week 7: The Final Stages of the Journey

Week 8: The Cross

Week 9: Resurrection

Week 10: New Beginnings

Conclusion: A Sense of Homecoming

Day 6: Resting prayer

During the first four days of each week you will be actively entering through your imagination into the meditation of the day. On the fifth day your focus will be on recalling the most striking things which came out of the previous four days.

At the centre of all of that is the truth that God loves each one of us deeply, wonderfully and unconditionally. So, on each Day 6 we will simply stay with and rest in that specific truth. Use the time you have set aside and just rest in the truth of God's love for you. Let him wash over you, hold you, immerse you.

On the journey to Iona I referred to in the Foreword I walked to the north end of the Island and sat on a black rock on a white sandy beach. Today this is a beautiful and peaceful place, but during the Viking raids of the ninth century this was also a place of bloodshed. I wrote in my journal:

> I have a sense of you holding me in your hands as I sit here looking over the beach. An oystercatcher and two sanderlings are running along the beach. The drizzle is coming and going and the waves are breaking on the white sand. You have brought me here and I am held. You always hold me, but here in this place and at this time I am especially conscious of this.

Then I wrote what I sensed Jesus saying to me in response:

> I have brought you to this place and this time, I am holding you. There is nothing you need to do except be still and enjoy my presence.

Fortunately, you don't have to go to the north end of Iona and sit in the drizzle to experience God holding you. He is doing just that already. Take time on each Day 6 to rest in his presence and let him take you wherever he sees fit.

These extracts from Gregory Boyd's book *Seeing is Believing* help to capture the essence of resting prayer:

> It is only when we cease from our striving and rest in the unconditional love of Christ that our soul begins to be nourished and restored. It is only then that we can experience a worth that attaches to our *being* and not simply our *doing* … The only goal of this time is for you to *just be you*, with all your imperfections, and let Christ *just be Christ* in all his perfection. It is a time just to rest in truth: the truth of who you are and who God is. And both are found in Jesus, who is fully God and fully human.[5]

The lead into each Day 6 contains material which I hope will help you enter a time of resting prayer. On some occasions it will be sufficient to sit in silence in the presence of the God who loves you. However, many of us find that when stopping and sitting still our minds continue to race on, following all kinds of leads and distractions.

There are various ways in which you can deal with distraction. One is to start with a single word or phrase and when your mind goes off at a tangent come back to that word or phrase as a way of re-engaging with God's presence. It could be the name 'Jesus' or a phrase such as 'I love your presence' or 'Be close to me now'.

---

5. Gregory A. Boyd, *Seeing is Believing* (See pages 104-105.)

On some occasions it may be helpful to play some quiet background instrumental music – something that helps you focus on the presence of God and is not a distraction in its own right. I've used *In the Stillness* by Eric Terlizzi (The Orchard) for myself and in small groups.

Some people may find that lighting a candle at the beginning of a time of resting prayer is helpful, or having a cross or some artwork as a focal point.

Experiment and find what is helpful to you, but I suggest keep it simple. The objective for this time is simply to soak in the presence of God.

It might help to identify and then put to one side the things that engage and concern you; they will still be there when you 'return'. Sometimes I have written down my concerns on small pieces of paper and placed them to one side, not to be revisited until the end of my prayer time.

You are there to rest in the presence of Jesus, to be held by him. Make yourself present to him as he is present to you. Relax into his love for you.

For many this is not an easy form of prayer; it can take time and practice to be able to slow down and just be in the presence of Jesus. But what could be better than that?

Day 7: Day off!

It's good to build variety into whatever spiritual discipline you are following. In undertaking the Ignatian Spiritual Exercises you are encouraged to take a day off every week. It's an opportunity to do something else.

So if you simply want to have a 'day off', that's fine. For those who would like some framework and content for Day 7, I've chosen to provide this in the form of a journey out from the place where you live and back again. If you find this material helpful then please use it, but just having a day off is fine as well.

Getting started

Begin by reading the Scripture passages and notes. As you engage with the material and questions for each day, see where the Holy Spirit takes you. Open up a conversation and see what Jesus has to say to you.

Couple your reading, meditation and prayer with journaling in order to capture and record your thoughts, impressions and those conversations with Jesus. If you can, each day take at least thirty to forty minutes, including journaling what you have seen, heard and experienced.

Take as much time as you need with all of this. If you find something that requires several days' attention, stay with it, don't rush on. Don't feel you have to complete the 'course' in ten weeks. You may also want to stop at various points, take a week off or longer. However, I would say that there is a benefit in keeping the momentum going. As you do that, the sense of friendship and sharing the journey builds.

I hope you find this Retreat helpful in your personal friendship and journey with Jesus.

The Ten Week Retreat

Week 1: Preparing for Your Journey

You are embarking on a journey with Jesus, joining him and taking part in the story of his life as recorded in the Gospels. How do you prepare for such an adventure? Most journeys work best with some degree of preparation, and this is no exception. Some of the ground has already been covered and you may have decided on the basics, for example, time commitment, a solo voyage or with a companion, how to fit this journey into the rest of your life.

Earlier in this book I introduced myself. I like to know who I'm travelling with, especially if my companion is a stranger. In a real sense you and I are taking this journey together. You know a little about me, but how often do you stop and ask a few questions about yourself? Who is the person starting this particular journey with Jesus? What are the pathways that have led you to this particular moment?

And then what about Jesus himself, how do you see him? Is he someone you aspire to know for the first time? Or someone you have travelled with over many years, and if that's the case, how is your relationship with him right now?

Let's start the journey with some preparation covering the above ground. I suggest that you spend the first day simply 'introducing' yourself to Jesus. Telling him who you are and why you want to travel with him through his story and on into yours. Then the next three days can be spent going into a little more detail, so that towards the end of this first week you have the sense that you are holding nothing back, and are happy to be fully known by him. Of course, Jesus already knows you more fully than you know or understand yourself. But the process of unpacking where you are at, in Jesus' presence, seems to help in freeing up our communication with him, and allows him to take the conversation further.

If you are in the process of exploring what faith in Jesus might look like for you, then I have the sense that Jesus especially welcomes and invites you to join him.

Day 1: Introducing yourself to Jesus

It's time to start. Keep this simple and imagine Jesus coming to the place where you are sitting as you read these words. Maybe invite him into the room, and imagine giving him a coffee. He's ready to travel and eager to get to know you better before setting out. Already you begin to sense his love for you as you sit together.

It's not important to imagine a lot of detail; just hold the idea that he is present, relaxing with you before you set off. Initiate the conversation; you could use some of the following prompts:

- Let me tell you a little about myself…
- This is why I want to take this particular journey with you…
- I'm hoping for this as we travel together…
- There are a few things that concern me…

Now use your journal to record the things you are saying to Jesus. He is interested in everything you have to say. You hold no surprises for him; he loves you unconditionally so feel free, you don't need to hold anything back.

If you are still in the early stages of exploring the possibility of a relationship with Jesus, then this is the place to begin. Tell him where you have got to in your search and the questions you are carrying.

- You may have the sense that Jesus is asking you some questions as well. If that's the case, then capture them in your journal.
- He may also have something to say or show you. Be open to where he takes you.

When you feel that the conversation is complete, thank him for his presence with you and his willingness to draw you into his journey, in the Gospel story, and today.

Day 2: Your faith journey so far

I hope that yesterday was a helpful first step. Today I'd like you to go a little further by reviewing your faith journey so far. In the time you have available, I suggest you focus on the following three areas:

1. Firstly identify the things that draw you towards God. For example, this could be meeting him in the narrative of the Bible, experiencing his presence in your daily life, in the lives of others, or in creation.
2. Next identify the things that have the opposite effect. For example, times when God seems distant, inaccessible.
3. Finally, in the light of the above, describe your current personal experience of God, however tentative that might be.

Journal what comes to mind; use short sentences and bullet points to get to the heart of your experience.

It's not uncommon to look back at times when God seemed more real, worship was reaching out and touching him, prayer was answered in tangible ways. But! What happened next and how has that left you feeling? Or maybe you are at an early stage in your journey when everything seems uncertain.

Bring the outline of your faith story to Jesus in prayer.

- Ask him where he was when you were facing the big issues of your life.

- Ask him to show you how your journey and his are linked together.

Take your time to listen and journal what he has to say.

Thank him for his presence with you and for the specific ways in which he is drawing you towards himself.

Day 3: Seasons of faith

Most people's faith journey is one of ups and downs rather than the smoothly ascending growth curve we might aspire to. I once watched some pelicans circling the same spot, gradually gaining height until they found a current of wind that sent them gliding towards their chosen destination. It can be like that, feeling that you are not really progressing, just marking time, going round and round. But then the wind of the Spirit comes and takes you on, perhaps to an unexpected destination.

The seasons of the year can be used as a template for understanding some of the stages your faith journey may pass through. For example:

- Spring – with its hopeful new beginnings can often feel vulnerable and uncertain.
- Summer – can bring warmth and abundance, and a sense of being in a good place.
- Autumn – a time of fruitfulness, tempered by the knowledge that winter is close.
- Winter – barren and sometimes stormy, but expectant.

Just a few words to describe some stages you may progress through, and not just once but possibly again and again. Hopefully, like the pelicans I saw, making some progress each time around.

Use this template of the seasons as a general guide to assess where you are right now. Don't worry if they don't seem to fit you exactly, use your own words to describe the season(s) that are relevant to you.

- What 'season' best describes your life with God at the present time?
- Are you surprised by your answer?
- Are you comfortable right now or do you want to move from where you are?

Maybe there are aspects of your life that are in the grip of winter, while others are fruitful.

Now think about the 'seasons' Jesus' life passed through – the springtime of his early life, the winter of his burial.

Speak to Jesus about the seasons you have passed through, where you find yourself right now, and how you feel about all of that. He might have something to say about his journey as well as about yours. Use your journal to capture what he says in reply.

Day 4: Your relationship with Jesus

I'm hoping that the last three days have provided you with some snapshots of your life taken from different angles. At the heart of each aspect of your life is your relationship with Jesus. What feeds and nurtures that relationship? What has the opposite effect? How has that changed over time as you have passed through different 'seasons'?

In amongst all the different aspects of life there is a place we call home, the place we live from. I want to suggest two different ways of living out our relationship with Jesus that shape the place we live from. I'm calling those two ways Function and Friendship. They can sit together happily but the question is, which one is home?

Close to the end of the time Jesus spent with his first disciples, he talked to them about the contrast between being a servant and a friend. They had been with him for three years, seen his miracles, listened to his teaching, and travelled on mission for him. Now as he is about to leave them he says:

> I no longer call you servants, because a servant does not know his master's business. Instead, I have called you friends, for everything that I learned from my Father I have made known to you. You did not choose me, but I chose you and appointed you so that you might go and bear fruit – fruit that will last … (John 15:15-16)

In the past servants often lived in their own quarters – below stairs or in a tied house. Their identity was tied to their function as servants. Jesus does not regard us as servants, but as family and friends. This is the place we live from – the family home. As we serve him and others, we are doing this as part of his family in friendship.

- Read Jesus' words in John 15:1-17. How would you describe the place you live from?
- How do you see yourself – as a servant or a friend?
- How does that make you feel?

Ask Jesus how he sees you; you might be surprised at what he says to you and where he takes you. Thank him that he is seeking to draw you into his friendship.

Day 5: Repetition

Use the time you have today to draw together the things that have stood out so far. As you do that, think about how this process of preparation has affected you; take note of your feelings.

You started this week by 'introducing' yourself to Jesus as a way of preparing for the ten-week journey. In the coming weeks you will enter into, and take part in, Jesus' own journey recorded in the Gospels, and like the first disciples, experience him drawing you further into his friendship.

Take your time in Jesus' presence and allow him to highlight whatever he wants you to see more clearly today.

- Maybe it's the season you see yourself in, or progressing towards?
- It could be the things that draw you towards him?
- Or maybe a sense of gratitude that wherever you are on your journey, he is alongside you giving you hope and inspiration.

Thank him for his willingness to travel with you through today and the rest of your life.

Day 6: Resting prayer

Each sixth day takes a different approach as explained in Chapter 2. Look back at some of the suggestions set out there and use whatever seems helpful today.

At the centre of everything is the truth that God loves each one of us deeply, wonderfully and unconditionally. So on each Day 6 simply stay with that specific truth. Use the time you have intentionally set aside and just rest in the truth of God's love for you. Let it wash over you, hold you, immerse you.

Today you might find this prayer from the *Iona Abbey Worship Book: Service of Quiet* helpful to begin with. You might like to imagine yourself in a quiet place of worship that you are familiar with, in company with others, or alone, entering God's presence.

Jesus, you commanded waves to be still and calmed a stormy sea. Quieten now my restless heart that I may find rest in you. I recognise the noises inside me and the noises around me. I acknowledge them, but seek here to know your presence in the midst of all that might distract me. So, now, I surrender for these moments my speech, knowing that beneath the silence is a deeper Word, and even when I say nothing, you are still listening. Ever listening, ever watchful, ever loving God, I rest in you.[6]

Remember that you are here to rest in the presence of Jesus, to be held by him. Make yourself present to him as he is present to you. Relax into his love for you during this short time.

---

6. The Iona Community, *Iona Abbey Worship Book* (Glasgow: Wild Goose Publications, 2016). (See pages 53-54.) Adapted for personal use.

Day 7: Day off!

Have a break and do something different of your choosing. Or you might like to engage with the following as a starting point:

Today why not go around the room(s) of the place you live in and imagine Jesus there with you.

When you have done that, return to the space where you have chosen to pray and invite him into the 'rooms' of your personal life. If you can, tell him there are no hidden corners that are out of bounds for him.

- How does it feel to give Jesus unfettered access to every part of your life?
- Speak to him about your feelings and capture the conversation in your journal.

Week 2: Preparing for Jesus' Journey

Last week you were largely focused on your own preparation. Introducing yourself to Jesus, and in the process seeing more clearly where you are starting from. I hope that was helpful. You covered a lot of ground and you may want to return to some the insights you gained and review them again at the end of the Retreat.

During this week we enter Jesus' own story. It's one that does not start with the angel meeting Mary, but can be traced back through the Old Testament. I'm not covering that ground here. I would like to start with Jesus' role in creation. In that way we can seek to engage with the immense mystery of God coming to our small but wonderful planet as a human. Then we will meet Mary and Joseph and witness the birth of Jesus.

Day 1: The Creator becomes a creature

Read Colossians 1:15-20

Paul was writing in a very different context to ours as regards understanding the universe, how it came into being, its size and complexity. In these verses he was not, however, addressing the science of creation but rather who is behind it and what it is for. In other words, he is dealing with a big question which people often come back to – why are we here?

There is scope here for going in many directions, but I would like you to focus simply on the mystery that lies behind Paul's words in verses 16 and 17. Today we know more about the universe than at any time in history, but still our knowledge is partial. The scale of God's creation is staggering, with more galaxies and stars that we could imagine. Then there is the other way of seeing creation as we go deeper into the structure of matter, down to subatomic particles. What we are beginning to understand about the fine-tuning and complexity of creation is astonishing.

Reflecting a few years ago I wrote in my journal about the 'sense that science is giving us greater insight into God's creative activity, we have a glimpse of the master craftsman at work shaping and setting the parameters of creation'. For some people scientific knowledge can replace God in their thinking. For me, it expands my vision of God; with each discovery I am given new insights into his creative activity. And it's not just about physics and cosmology; as I was reflecting I also thought about some of my grandchildren, including Amelie, just three weeks old at the time, and her two brothers, also wonderful expressions of God's creation. I am grateful to be part of God's handiwork.

Read again verses 16 and 17:

> [He] is the image of the invisible God, the firstborn over all creation. For in him all things were created: things … visible and invisible … all things have been created through him and for him. He is before all things, and in him all things hold together.

It may help to imagine standing outside with Jesus on a dark night with a razor-sharp view of the sky. Maybe he is pointing something out to you, a shooting star, or the glow from the Milky Way.

- You might have some questions, or is it just enough to be standing alongside him?
- How does that feel, standing next to the creator of the universe?
- Do you need to have all the answers? Are there times when you can live with mystery because you are in the presence of Jesus?

Go a little deeper and use your journal to capture your thoughts and what you are experiencing.

Thank God for his creative power, for the fact that anything exists and that you can experience life here on planet Earth. Thank him for this moment in time when you can relate to the Creator of the universe as a friend.

Day 2: Mary

Read Luke 1:26-38

The Ignatian Spiritual Exercises, which provide much of my inspiration here, are rooted within Catholic tradition. Within my tradition we respect Mary but do not give her the same prominence. Probably we are overreacting to what we see as an overreaction.

As you read Luke's account and consider the incarnation, can you sense the deep connection and love Jesus had, and still has, for Mary, his mother?

While entering this story I realised how little I think about Mary, yet she was such a special person to Jesus. I thought of Jesus as a bundle of cells within Mary's womb.

Read Luke's account again and imagine yourself as a bystander, surprised by what you have just seen and heard!

- Can you sense what Mary felt after the angel left her?
- Can you feel the contrast between the excitement of being caught up in the immensity of God's purpose and the vulnerability of working this out in real life, in the culture of her day?

- Can you identify with that contrast in your own experience? Thank God for the willingness of Mary to become part of the greatest story ever experienced on earth. Think about your own willingness and desire to be part of that story as well.

Day 3: Joseph

Read Matthew 1: 18-25

We know so little about Joseph, and yet he too was such an important person in Jesus' early life. Reading Matthew 1:18-25, I reflected on his love for Mary – he wants to avoid her being hurt or damaged. His culture pointed towards their separation, until God stepped in and showed him the bigger picture through a couple of dreams.

In this part of the Gospel story we can see the importance of the 'bigger picture'. Seeing that picture keeps us in tune with God at those times when we can get focused on custom and the normal way of handling things.

As I spent time in this story I felt Jesus showing me that both Mary and Joseph were able to set aside 'normal practice' because they were caught up in what he was doing. Did Mary and Joseph see the whole of God's 'big picture'? No, it unfolded for them, but they knew they were living within it.

- Speak to Jesus about how your life and circumstances fit within the context of his 'big picture'.
- See what he says to you about his calling for you and how friendship will enable you to live within that 'big picture' as it unfolds for you.

Round off your prayer time by thanking God that you are part of his story.

Day 4: Birth

Read Luke 2:1-20

Do you sometimes experience God taking you places you prefer not to go? The journey Mary and Joseph took just before Jesus was born was not of their choosing. Think of a 130km (80 mile) route you are familiar with and then imagine walking and riding that just before giving birth. As I read Luke's Gospel, I thought about carrying Jesus to places not of my choosing, to people who seem closed to God's love.

Mary and Joseph were drawn into what God was doing. They didn't initiate, but they were open and willing to play their part. Your part and mine may seem small in comparison, but who knows where God will take us next?

The shepherds were drawn in, taken by surprise, overwhelmed. Then the moment passed, they were back on their cold hillside, but changed by what they had experienced.

This is familiar ground, but entering into it as a bystander, or one of the visitors, can bring the story to life in a new way. A good friend of mine did just that in his prayer time; standing to one side he watched the comings and goings of the visitors. Then to his surprise Mary walked over to him and handed him the baby to hold while she did something else. My friend was overwhelmed by the 'experience' of holding Jesus; even in telling me the story, he was quite emotional. Then to his relief Mary returned and retrieved the baby.

Place yourself in the scene described by Luke and be open to what God wants to show you.

Jesus was born at the right time and place.

- What about the people you and I desire to see born again?
- Mary was 'full' of Jesus, heavily pregnant. How full of Jesus am I?
- Can he be born in others unless you and I are full of him?

Thank God for the wonder of the incarnation.

Day 5: Repetition

During this week you have witnessed the birth of a baby, an amazing event. I remember well the births of my three daughters; it is a truly awesome experience. The Gospel introduces us to Mary and Joseph, key people in Jesus' early life. The story contains a profound mystery, the creator and sustainer of the universe born as a human being.

- Use the time you have today to draw together the things that have stood out to you so far.
- As you do that, see how this process has affected you. Take note of your feelings.

Take your time in Jesus' presence and allow him to highlight whatever he wants you to see more clearly today.

Day 6: Resting prayer

Each sixth day takes a different approach as explained in Chapter 2. Look back at some of the suggestions set out there and use whatever seems most helpful today.

At the centre of everything is the truth that God loves each one of us deeply, wonderfully and unconditionally. So on each Day 6 simply stay with that specific truth. Use the time you have intentionally set aside and just rest in the truth of God's love for you. Let it wash over you, hold you, immerse you.

Today you might like to place yourself in the scene described in Song of Songs 2:8-13, NIV 1984 version. This book can be read in a number of ways. At its heart it conveys, in beautiful imagery, something of God's love for each one of us. Read this passage slowly and allow Jesus to speak the words the lover speaks to his beloved, to you. See where he takes you.

> Listen! My lover!
> Look! Here he comes,
> leaping across the mountains,
> bounding over the hills.
> My lover is like a gazelle or a young stag.
> Look! There he stands behind our wall,
> gazing through the windows,
> peering through the lattice.
> My lover spoke and said to me,
> 'Arise, my darling,
> my beautiful one, and come with me.
> See! The winter is past;

the rains are over and gone.
Flowers appear on the earth;
The season of singing has come,
the cooing of doves
is heard in our land.
The fig-tree forms its early fruit;
the blossoming vines spread their fragrance.
Arise, come, my darling;
my beautiful one, come with me.

You are here to rest in the presence of Jesus, to be held by him. Make yourself present to him as he is present to you. Relax into his love for you during this short time.

Day 7: Day off!

Have a break and do something different of your choosing. Or you might like to engage with the following as a starting point:

If it seems helpful, why not take the idea of inviting Jesus into the physical place you live in and the 'rooms' of your personal life a stage further. Imagine walking with Jesus around the community where you live. If the weather is good and this seems appropriate you could spend this prayer time walking in your immediate neighbourhood, praying for people in the houses you walk past, and in the businesses and shops. Or just imagine that walk as you sit at home.

Week 3: Out of Security and into Vulnerability

During this week we encounter Jesus in the transition from his life in a small village, working in the family business, to the uncertainty of beginning his public ministry. So far you've been an observer, looking in from the outside. Now your journey together through the story begins. It starts in the family home and the workshop, then gathers pace as you witness Jesus' baptism and perhaps take the same step for yourself.

After witnessing Jesus' temptation, you see him choosing his first disciples. As this week unfolds you will become increasingly engaged in Jesus' life and ministry.

Day 1: Growing up

Read Luke 2:41-52

We know very little about Jesus' childhood. His father was a carpenter (or maybe a builder); he lived in a small village, along with his brothers and sisters. He grew up in the context of Jewish culture and faith. It's safe to assume he was working alongside Joseph learning his trade during his adolescence.

Even with these basic details it's not too difficult to begin this journey with Jesus by imagining being with him at home and working alongside him in the carpenter's workshop. Standing alongside, smell the fresh shavings littering the floor; hear the sound of metal tools working along the grain of the wood. This is a place full of activity, people collecting finished goods and delivering materials. Hard, demanding and skilful work, in company with others, conversation flying back and forth across the shop floor as pieces of wood are shaped and pinned together.

Luke's account describes one incident in Jesus' childhood. Does it give you a feel for what it must have been like for him as he grew up in a normal everyday family, yet knowing who he really was?

Think about your twenties; what were (or are) you doing? Maybe you were beginning to discover who you are, and think about the purpose of your life.

- Now join Jesus in your imagination at the workbench (or on a building site).
- What does it feel like to be working alongside Jesus, making or building things?

- Ask him what was it like being in fellowship with his heavenly Father at the same time as learning a trade and being part of a family and local community.

As you round off in prayer, thank God for your own circle of family, friends and colleagues. People you may take for granted who form the backdrop for your life. People you can bring Jesus to as you meet them in ordinary daily life.

Day 2: Baptism

Read Matthew 3:13-17

I imagine the family home in Nazareth and the carpenter's workshop as places of security and familiarity. Matthew tells us that the time came when Jesus was ready to step out from the anonymity he had enjoyed in the workshop to embrace the vulnerability and risks of the open road; teaching, healing, being recognised, loved and hated.

What was it like for Jesus to take that step? If you are willing to join him in moving from security to vulnerability as you travel together, how does that feel? And is friendship one of the things that draws you to join Jesus on his journey?

Read again Matthew 3:13-17 and as you do, take some time to imagine yourself on the banks of the River Jordan. There are crowds there listening to John and waiting to be baptised by him. There's an excitement in the air, God is doing something new. Watch as John finally agrees to baptise Jesus, and together they go down into the water. See the Spirit descend on Jesus like a dove, hear the voice from heaven affirming Jesus and declaring God's love. This is such a rich picture, take your time, get as close in as you can.

- You might want to embrace Jesus as he comes out of the water.
- Imagine it's your turn to be baptised. If you are willing, go down into the water and take John's hand. Allow him to immerse you and bring you out of the water again. How does that feel?
- Speak to Jesus as you both stand on the riverbank together, soaking wet.

As you close this time of prayer, thank Jesus for inviting you to take part in his story, and for drawing you into his friendship. Already you've come a long way together from the security of the carpenter's workshop.

Day 3: Temptation

Read Luke 4:1-13

Jesus was led by the Spirit straight from baptism to his temptation in the desert. Here you are simply an observer; you cannot help Jesus in any way. But having come this far with him, neither can you walk away and leave him. There are times when all we can do is to be present, with him and with others, and that's enough.

As you think about Luke's account, imagine yourself sitting on a rock in the desert watching and listening. Jesus is being tested not in areas of weakness but in areas of strength and identity. If you doubt your identity, everything begins to collapse around you.

- Have there been times when you have felt unsure about who you really are?

- Or times when you question what you are here for?
- Ask Jesus to tell you who he thinks you are, and how he sees you.

Listen carefully to Jesus as he tells you who you are. You might be surprised by what he has to say to you. Whatever he says, allow yourself time for his words to sink in deeply.

In prayer, thank Jesus for allowing you an insight into his times of vulnerability and testing. Thank him for being present with you when you experience similar seasons.

Day 4: First disciples

Read John 1:43-51

Discipleship starts when you encounter Jesus and begin to follow him. John provides us with a striking story of how Nathanael met and decided to follow Jesus. Place yourself in Nathanael's shoes and use his conversation with Jesus as a template for one of your own. See where this takes you, what happens, what words are exchanged.

John is not specific about the place where Nathanael met Jesus, so you could make it somewhere you are familiar with. Wherever it is, imagine you are there now. Look around and take in your surroundings.

Now imagine Jesus walking towards you. Don't worry if you don't have a lot of detail. You recognise him as he approaches and he knows who you are, just as he knew Nathanael. He is pleased to see you, he greets you by name. Imagine Jesus doing that to you right now.

- What do you say to him and what does he say in reply?

Nathanael declared what he believed about Jesus and in return Jesus made some remarkable statements.

- Does Jesus have some promises for you that will take you into the next stage of your life with him?

Stay in Jesus' presence – he knows you and all the things that have led you to this point in your life. He loves and welcomes you.

Review what has taken place and capture that in your journal. Thank Jesus for drawing you into discipleship and for the promises he makes to you.

Day 5: Repetition

After the time of growing up comes the challenge of stepping out and embracing the journey with Jesus. Where will that take you? You have no idea, it is a journey into uncertainty and vulnerability.

- Review the previous four days and reflect on your feelings about what Jesus has been saying to you.
- Think about the ways in which you feel connected to him and his journey.

Day 6: Resting prayer

Each sixth day takes a different approach as explained in Chapter 2. Look back at some of the suggestions set out there and use whatever seems helpful today.

At the centre of everything is the truth that God loves each one of us deeply, wonderfully and unconditionally. So on each Day 6 simply stay with that specific truth. Use the time you have intentionally set aside and just rest in the truth of God's love for you. Let it wash over you, hold you, immerse you.

Today you might like to use this incident at the beginning of Jesus' ministry as your lead in to resting prayer:

> The next day John was there again with two of his disciples. When he saw Jesus passing by, he said, 'Look, the Lamb of God!' When the two disciples heard him say this, they followed Jesus. Turning round, Jesus saw them following and asked, 'What do you want?' They said, 'Rabbi' (which means 'Teacher'), 'where are you staying?' 'Come,' he replied, 'and you will see.' (John 1:35-39)

Accept Jesus' invitation to you to come, and see where he takes you.

You are here to rest in the presence of Jesus, to be held by him. Make yourself present to him as he is present to you. Relax into his love for you during this short time.

Day 7: Day off!

Have a break and do something different of your choosing. Or you might like to engage with the following as a starting point:

Why not take last week's neighbourhood prayer walk a stage further? Think about the wider context within which you live, your local hospitals and schools, the local council, the main places where people work in your area. Imagine visiting each of those places with Jesus, and as you do so, ask him to bless the people working there.

Week 4: Engaging in What Jesus is Doing, Then and Now

Last week you entered the early years of Jesus' life. With him you left the security of the family home, witnessed his baptism and temptation, and the calling of his first disciples. It was an important transitional week. Now it's time to engage with Jesus as he moves out into the wider community. You will witness him healing the sick, teaching the crowds, confronting injustice. As you enter into this week's encounters, allow Jesus to draw you into what he is doing. Be aware of your feelings as this happens.

As we join Jesus on his journey today we will begin to see things as he sees them. This will include things that delight him (such as making sure a wedding celebration is a great occasion, or giving someone his sight), and those causing him offence.

Day 1: Water into wine

Read John 2:1-11

John tells us that this was the first of Jesus' miraculous signs. We don't know anything about the bride and groom but they must have been well-known to Jesus and his family. Cana in Galilee is about 6km (nearly 4 miles) from Nazareth.

You might like to enter this story as one of the servants. There's a problem and you can't fix it, the wine has run out and the wedding feast is in full swing. There is nothing you can do, but Mary seems to have an idea. She takes the problem to Jesus, and without telling him what to do, or asking for anything specific, she just lets him know there's a problem.

As you listen to that conversation, what are you thinking? What could Jesus possibly do about this? Why is Mary even mentioning it?

Jesus' response to Mary is surprising, 'why do you involve me?' but Mary seems to know something you don't and she tells you to do whatever Jesus tells you.

What happens next seems crazy. You and your fellow servants are told to fill the ceremonial washing jars with water. This is a big ask; there are six jars and each holds 90-135 litres (20-30 gallons).

It takes a lot of time and effort for you and your colleagues to do this. You ask yourself, 'Why are we doing this? It's not the right time for the water in these jars to be used, and what has this got to do with the lack of wine?' You are a servant so you get on with what Jesus tells you to do. And you do a good job; the jars are full to the brim.

Now Jesus asks you to do something that makes you feel insecure and vulnerable. Take some of the water to the master of the feast to taste. You know this is just water; what is the master going to say to you when he tastes it?

- Take some time to reflect, still in the presence of Jesus, on times when he has asked you to do something that seemed crazy or pointless.
- Or times when you were given something from Jesus to say to someone else and felt vulnerable as you delivered it.
- And those times when what you were asked to do seemed so impossible you just walked away.

Bring your thoughts to Jesus in prayer; what does he have to say to you? And is there something specific he wants you to do in the coming week?

Day 2: Healing the blind

Read: Mark 10:46-52

Reading the stories about Jesus healing the blind makes me think about my own areas of blindness. Mostly I see things from my own perspective and not his. I can be deeply indifferent to the many things I don't wish to see.

Entering this familiar story of the healing of Bartimaeus takes us to a key question from Jesus: 'What do you want me to do for you?'

Before you get to that question, take some time to enter this story, maybe as someone on a journey towards Jericho meeting Jesus as he leaves that city. If this is helpful you could fill in some of the detail that Mark takes for granted – it's hot, dusty and noisy on the road, there are many others making a similar journey, some with children, others driving animals loaded with goods for the market, some rich people and some very poor.

As you approach the city you see in the distance a group of people coming out of the gate walking in your direction. You draw closer to them; they are clustered around one individual who is leading the way. He is walking purposefully and talking to those closest to him.

The group are about to pass close to you when suddenly someone is shouting so loudly that his voice reaches over all the other noises you can hear: 'Jesus, Son of David, have mercy on me!' Some of the people nearby are telling him to be quiet but he shouts out even louder. You can feel a tension in the air and wonder what's going to happen.

Jesus stops, and the crowd of followers with him. He says 'Call him' and then asks, 'What do you want me to do for you?' Bartimaeus says, 'Rabbi, I want to see.' Jesus with his eyes fixed on him says, 'Go … your faith has healed you.' Immediately he can see, he shouts out and leaps into the air. The group of followers and bystanders go wild with excitement, praising God.

You are also amazed and as the crowd surrounds Bartimaeus in excitement, Jesus moves to one side and comes towards you. You are rooted to the spot, and then he speaks your name – and asks you the same question: 'What do you want me to do for you?'

- Imagine he's asking you that question right now.
- What do you say in reply?

Capture the conversation in your journal. Thank him for calling you over as he did Bartimaeus, and that he wants to know the answer to that question from you as well.

Days 3 and 4: Jesus' reaction to unjust situations

The following two stories illustrate Jesus' reaction to unjust situations. When I come to passages such as these in the Gospels, I need to ask myself – do I feel the same level of intensity as I see in Jesus as he engages with injustice? Often I just shrug; it's bad but what can I do about it? How can I bring change in unjust situations? What more could you or I be doing?

Day 3: Clearing the temple

Read John 2:12-25

In this story we encounter Jesus clearing the temple of people selling animals for sacrifice and changing money. He had been there many times before and seen this going on. Now it was his time to take a stand. If you had been there observing him, would you have been taken aback and shocked?

Reading this passage I had the sense of Jesus saying to me: 'If we are to walk more closely in friendship, as you desire, you will also have to engage with injustice as you see me doing so. As in all things, see what I am doing and when I am doing it, and take up the causes and cases that I bring before you.'

Faced with a world full of injustice and exploitation, what do you do? It's easy to feel overwhelmed and become passive.

I can see how Jesus' encouragement to take up the causes that he places before us works out in practice. About eighteen years ago an Iranian asylum seeker started coming to the church I'm a member of in Newcastle. He brought many of his friends and before long we had a significant group of Iranians linking themselves to the church. Over time we helped many of them through the asylum process, confronting the injustice they were often subjected to along the way. We felt frustration and anger at the way they were treated. Part of our response was to set up a charity, Action Foundation, which in 2018 supported 1,413 refugees, asylum seekers and other migrants through its housing and language projects.[7]

Looking back, I think we took up a cause that Jesus placed before us. We experienced his anger at injustice, but also his compassion and determination to make a difference.

- What are the injustices that Jesus is bringing before you?
- What causes can you engage with, personally or within the community you are part of?
- Maybe there is just one individual whose cause you want to champion?
- Where could engaging with injustice lead you?

---

7. For the latest information see the Action Foundation Website: https://actionfoundation.org.uk (accessed 19.6.19).

Take time in the presence of Jesus who cleared the temple with a whip of cords. Ask him to help you as you think through these questions; see where he takes you.

Day 4: The woman caught in the act of adultery

Read John 8:1-11

This story highlights a different aspect of injustice. A woman caught in the act of adultery is brought before Jesus to test him, not out of any concern for justice. The woman was treated as the sole offender – where was the man? Jesus' response to those wanting to condemn the woman was radical, cutting across the religious and cultural practice of the day. He wants to release those who are victimised so that repentance and a new start are possible.

As you read this story imagine yourself edging forward into the crowd surrounding Jesus as the incident unfolds. Jesus had come to the temple to teach the people, now he is confronted with anger and accusation. He takes his time; he is not about to be manipulated or pressurised. Watch him as he writes on the ground as the barrage of demands continues. Then he straightens himself and speaks with authority and compassion.

Listen to his words again and ask yourself – is anyone in a position to condemn another? And then his words to the woman – 'neither do I condemn you … Go now and leave your life of sin.' She is challenged to make a radical change, but not condemned as she would have been by her accusers.

- Are you sometimes quick to condemn and slow to forgive?

- Bring to mind someone you know, or have heard about, who is a victim of unjust and unloving behaviour.
- Can you redress the balance by bringing love, acceptance, the possibility of repentance, and a new beginning into their lives?

In prayer, thank Jesus for his radical approach to injustice and ask him to help you see clearly how you can make this the way you live.

Day 5: Repetition

This week we have looked at four very different incidents. Making sure a wedding party was a great success, healing a blind man, responding to different unjust situations.

- Review the last four days and reflect on your feelings about what Jesus has been saying to you, and the way in which you feel connected to him and his journey.
- In particular, consider your feelings about Jesus' engagement in unjust situations.

Day 6: Resting prayer

Each sixth day takes a different approach as explained in Chapter 2. Look back at some of the suggestions set out there and use whatever seems helpful today.

At the centre of everything is the truth that God loves each one of us deeply, wonderfully and unconditionally. So on each Day 6 simply stay with that specific truth. Use the time you have intentionally set aside and just rest in the truth of God's love for you. Let it wash over you, hold you, immerse you.

Last week I suggested using Jesus' invitation to 'come … and … see' as the lead in to you time of resting prayer. A little further into John's Gospel we read of Jesus' meeting with Nathanael, who is surprised that Jesus knows him before they have met. We looked at that story last week. Why not open today's time of resting prayer by reminding yourself that God knows you fully? Maybe ask him to show you how he sees you as your lead in to prayer.

You are here to rest in the presence of Jesus, to be held by him. Make yourself present to him as he is present to you. Relax into his love for you during this short time.

Day 7: Day off!

Have a break and do something different of your choosing. Or you might like to engage with the following as a starting point:

If you are finding this ever-widening journey helpful, why not go forward another step today and pray for your nation? Do this imagining Jesus present in each of the contexts you pray for. Start with the national government, the leader of your nation, its ministers and civil servants. Imagine Jesus in the seat of government, sitting in on a debate. Ask him to bless all those who lead your nation. See if he leads you into more specific areas of prayer and follow him there.

Week 5: Walking Closely Together

During my journey through the Ignatian Spiritual Exercises a number of ideas and phrases kept returning to me – and continue to do so. One was Jesus saying to me: 'Keep in step with me, don't rush ahead or fall behind.' Walking in step with Jesus keeps me in touch with what he is doing and where he is going. I'm taking my lead from him. There's companionship in the journey, and that's how friendship grows.

During this week we will continue walking with Jesus through the Gospel story witnessing his miracles and for the first time begin to take part in them as well.

Day 1: Being a gift bearer

Read: Luke 9:10-17

As you read through this familiar passage, put yourself into the story and imagine that you were present when Jesus fed the 5,000 (probably more like 15,000 with the women and children). See yourself as one of the disciples taking part in the miracle by helping to distribute the bread and fish.

Take a few minutes to get into the story, read it again slowly. Can you imagine the crowds gathered in groups of fifty, sitting and talking together? They have been in Jesus' presence, heard him teaching but now they are hungry and wondering what will happen next. The disciples are also unsure and you can pick up their concern from Luke's account. Place yourself there, sense the atmosphere and the disciples' feelings.

Now Jesus takes what he has been given – five loaves of bread and two fish. He gives thanks for these gifts as you and the other disciples gather round him. Then you see him begin to divide them, putting them first into the disciples' hands and then yours to give to the people. You see him giving out more and more and still he has the bread and fish in his hands. You carry what you have been given and share with the fifty you are serving. You come back again and again, as do the other disciples. Each time as you return to Jesus more is given for you to give again. As you do this you realise you are not just witnessing but taking part in a great miracle.

- Think back to occasions when Jesus told you to do something without letting you know what he was intending to do next.
- How did you feel – fine because he asked you, or a bit scared?
- What is it like to be a gift bearer, taking what Jesus is putting into your hands to give to others?

Talk to Jesus about how it feels to be a gift bearer for him in this story, and in your normal everyday life. Use your journal and listen to what he has to say in reply.

Postscript

A good friend, Maggie Raja, told me the story of a similar miracle of multiplication which her husband, Peterus, took part in, literally as a gift bearer. It happened in a remote area of Sarawak, the Malaysian part of the island of Borneo. Over many years, Peterus sought to help the Penan, one of the last tribes in Sarawak with members still living as nomadic hunter-gatherers.

On this occasion, Peterus and others had arranged a Christian gathering for the Penan, not knowing how many people would come. They had prepared what they thought would be sufficient food, but to their surprise a much larger number turned up.

They served the food from a large pan and as they did so, knowing it was not sufficient, it just kept coming; there was plenty for everyone.

Day 2: Lazarus

Read John 11:1-44

There are many aspects of this miracle we could look at; in the time you have available I would like you to focus on the issue of keeping in step with Jesus.

Jesus knew that Lazarus was going to die and that he could prevent that happening, but he chose to wait before setting off. Not surprisingly the disciples didn't grasp what was going on. They were confused about what Jesus was telling them and apprehensive about what he intended to do. Lazarus' sisters and the local community were also confused – 'if you had been here [he] would not have died'.

In 2013 I came close to death as I experienced a heart attack and a cardiac arrest. Two days before that happened, I had one of the most vivid dreams of my life in which I saw myself swimming in a rough sea about to be swamped by a tsunami-scale wave. The dream closely matched the heart attack experience; including waking up alive with a start, both in bed at home and in hospital after the defibrillator had done its job! The dream made me aware that Jesus knew the heart attack was coming, and in our subsequent conversations he graciously showed me how he was with me as the events unfolded.

Jesus knew Lazarus was going to die, he knew I was about to have a heart attack. Both Lazarus and I were granted some 'extra time,' but I fully, and sadly, realise that's not everyone's experience.

This story takes us deep, into life and death situations. Recently four good friends I have prayed for have died. I was able to share a little in their last stages of life and witnessed Jesus sharing that journey with them as well. I've included John's story at the end of this book.

Keeping in step with Jesus – how difficult the disciples, sisters and the local community found this in the story of Lazarus. Take some time now to think about people you care about who are at risk.

- You might want to ask Jesus: 'Why didn't you come sooner?'
- Do you find it easy or hard to keep in step with what you perceive Jesus doing, or not doing?
- What is God saying to you about the difficult things you are facing?

Close this prayer time by bringing the people and situations you are carrying to Jesus in the light of what he is saying to you.

Day 3: The Good Samaritan

Read Luke 10:25-37
While this is a parable rather than an event in Jesus' life, it takes us to the heart of what it means to walk in step with him. Take a few minutes to put yourself in the shoes of the Samaritan. He was on a journey, getting on with his life and not expecting or wanting to be involved in rescuing someone. It sounds from the story that he was not poor, he had sufficient resources to stay at an inn, and had some work or business to complete. He was probably a busy person.

Now imagine yourself setting out on your 'journey' of a normal, typical day. Include in that some of what you are planning for the rest of today, or tomorrow. Think about your priorities and pressure points and how much or little capacity you have for unplanned interruptions.

Return to the parable in your imagination, but this time you are walking down the road with Jesus. You are in conversation with him, telling him what you are doing today, asking for his help (just like a normal prayer time). Now unexpectedly you see a man in the ditch. You turn to Jesus; what is he going to do? Imagine that he crosses over to help. Can you carry on walking, following after your own priorities, when you see what Jesus is doing?

Now imagine that in the middle of your normal day there's some unexpected and unwelcome interruption. But you are still walking along with Jesus. You look over to see what he is going to do. Can you join in, even though it may be inconvenient and costly?

- Do you find it difficult to keep in step with Jesus because you are focused on your own agenda and what you are seeking to achieve?
- Is it sometimes much easier to pass by on the other side, because it's not your problem?
- How does friendship with Jesus change things?

Speak to Jesus openly about the times when you struggle to keep in step with him.

As an aside I think that seeing things through Jesus' eyes makes all the difference. When reflecting on this story I felt Jesus saying to me:

You are still quite self-focused. I am part of that focus, but you are still mostly at the centre. Our friendship will change that as you learn to walk more closely with me. Believe me, I am walking alongside you and I have a smile on my face and not a frown.

This is a new way of seeing things, not necessarily your default position, but learned chosen behaviour.

Day 4: Sent out

Read Luke 10:1-24

This passage marks another important transition in the disciples' journey with Jesus. He was now ready to commission them to go out ahead of him and prepare his way. They went in pairs. There were seventy-two of them, a big step beyond the initial twelve.

They had specific tasks – to heal the sick and tell people about the kingdom in the places that Jesus was about to visit. The disciples were making progress, first seeing Jesus heal the sick and teach, then being involved when he was present, and now going out in pairs without him.

Today imagine yourself as one of those sent out. You might like to choose someone you know as a companion. Rather than seeking to enter the villages in Palestine, go to the places where Jesus is sending you today – places you are familiar with, people you know as well as others as yet unknown.

- What did engaging in this kind of mission feel like for the first disciples? What does it feel like to you?

- In prayer bring to Jesus the people and places you are reaching out to for him.
- Ask him how you can best prepare the way for him.

As you pray ask Jesus what he is doing, or going to do, and how you can join in.

This is challenging, but he will be encouraging you all the time as he did his first disciples.

Day 5: Repetition

Review the previous four days and reflect on your feelings about what Jesus has been saying to you, and the way in which you feel connected to him and his journey.

- Think about how difficult it can be to keep in step.
- Reflect on times when nothing seems to be going to plan, or when Jesus is not responding in the way you expect or hope for.
- How do you feel about being sent out?

Day 6: Resting prayer

Each sixth day takes a different approach as explained in Chapter 2. Look back at some of the suggestions set out there and use whatever seems helpful today.

At the centre of everything is the truth that God loves each one of us deeply, wonderfully and unconditionally. So on each Day 6 we will simply stay with that specific truth. Use the time you have intentionally set aside and just rest in the truth of God's love for you. Let it wash over you, hold you, immerse you.

As a lead in to resting prayer today you could read the story of Elijah's encounter with God in a mountain cave, in 1 Kings 19:11-13. The context is one of great conflict, heavy responsibility and stress. Elijah intentionally escapes to a remote place, and there he hears God speaking to him in a 'gentle whisper'.

Imagine the place where you are praying today as remote; that might help you to screen out the distractions you are facing. Stay in that 'remote' place and as you rest in Jesus' presence see if there is a gentle whisper that you can hear in the silence.

You are here to rest in the presence of Jesus, to be held by him. Make yourself present to him as he is present to you. Relax into his love for you during this short time.

Day 7: Day off!

Have a break and do something different of your choosing. Or you might like to engage with the following as a starting point:

Continuing the widening journey today and in the coming weeks you could use this time to focus on the challenges faced by humanity on the global scale. You could start by bringing some of the world's conflict zones to Jesus. He lived in an occupied territory, where authority was imposed brutally. Bring to mind conflicts you are aware of and stand with Jesus in those places. Begin to see what he sees as you look around. Talk to him about what you are experiencing; ask him to bring peace.

Week 6: Themes

At the midway point of the Retreat, this week will be different as we explore four themes drawn from my experience of journeying with Jesus through the Ignatian Spiritual Exercises.

Day 1: Image and reality

How do we engage with the mystery that is God? Part way through the Exercises I spent time reflecting on my images of God, and how they had changed during the different stages of my life. I listed some of the images I find particularly life-giving. God is my creator, companion and parent. He is someone full of love, life and purpose. I now see that my headings focused on my emotional connection to God, rather than being a list of his attributes and character. I could sit down and from the Bible, make another inventory of the rich and varied images it contains – redeemer, Saviour, Lord, midwife, mother, father for example.

During my prayer time I had a sense of Jesus saying:

> Images such as these convey meaning and will help you understand your relationship with me. Use them for what they are, images that provide a hint of a greater reality. You are not living in or through an image but in the reality it seeks to describe. Walk with me today as your creator, companion and parent. Bring to me the things that disturb you and live in the presence of who I am.'

Jesus reveals the image of God. In conversation with Philip, Jesus tells him 'Anyone who has seen me has seen the Father' (John 14:9). Jesus is 'the image of the invisible God' (Colossians 1:15).

Images used in the Bible have a vital purpose – 'to act as a vehicle to help us into a relationship with the God who is beyond definition, beyond category and beyond image' (Philip Endean).[8] Images are not intended to become an end in themselves; their purpose is to lead us into relationship. God is always beyond images and the framework they provide. As we begin to describe him we realise he is also beyond description.

If God begins to show you more of himself, can you cope with that? The relationship between Jesus and the religious leaders of his day, and even a cursory overview of Church history, shows that people easily get stuck in one set of images or concepts. They stay there rather than allowing God to reveal the greater mystery of what that image or concept is pointing towards.

---

8. Philip Endean noted during a course at St Beuno's, North Wales, 2016, and included with his permission.

Imaginative Prayer is particularly helpful in this context. It uses images as a means of connecting us to Jesus himself. The image leads us to the reality of Jesus. Imaginative Prayer can 'enable us to experience truth' (Gregory Boyd).[9]

- Take some time now to reflect on your images of God. Make a list in your journal.
- Have the images you find helpful broadened or narrowed over the years?
- Are some of the images that have helped you in the past no longer life-giving?
- Is God revealing more of himself to you in fresh images?

Round off this prayer time by thanking God for revealing himself most fully in Jesus. Thank him for what you have come to see already and for his willingness to take you further.

Day 2: Inner freedom

Further into my journey through the Ignatian Spiritual Exercises I reflected on how to enjoy the many good things that God has given me, including relationships and possessions, without the need to own, manipulate or control.

Ignatius placed considerable emphasis on letting go of genuinely good things that can so easily possess us. That is not too surprising when we remember that the Jesuit Order, which he conceived and founded, is built on a life of poverty, chastity and obedience.

I started by listing the people and possessions I most love. I

---

9. Gregory A. Boyd, *Seeing is Believing* (See page 72).

thought of my wife, Nicky, and our three daughters, now with families of their own. Yes, I was able to release our daughters in their late teens; I have no desire to own or control them and probably thanks to that our relationships remain loving and open.

In 2013 my heart attack showed me how quickly and unexpectedly life can be taken away. That experience made me realise that all things are a pure gift, to be held lightly and with generosity.

All of that said, what about the people and things I still surround myself with, do I own them or do they own me?

Maybe like me you could list the people and possessions you most love – could you let them go? How would that feel?

Ask yourself:

- Do I seek to control or own the (named) people that I love?
- The place where I live, my resources, the things that surround me, do they own me?
- If they were stripped away, would that matter?
- My ability and health, if I became limited (or more limited) in what I can do, how would that affect me?

Imagine Jesus sitting with you at a table as you work through these questions. Ask him to speak to you about what 'inner freedom' could look like for you.

Day 3: A refuge for others

Your friendship with Jesus can become a place of refuge for others. Living from a place of friendship with Jesus opens up new possibilities. During one of my prayer times I had a sense of Jesus saying:

Keep an open heart towards everyone you encounter, I have space for each of them, give them some of your space on my behalf. Let them enter the place you occupy, the place you are living from, and bless them. That place will enlarge over time and provide refuge for more and more people. As I change you, you will become a place of refuge and healing to many, a place in which I choose to meet others.

God brings us to a good place in himself, in part so that we can welcome and bring his blessing to others. This can be expressed in so many ways – having someone needing a roof over their head to stay in your home, sharing hospitality over a meal, conversation over a coffee, helping tidy someone's house for them. It includes many everyday expressions but there's more than that. It's also about sharing the place you are living from, in friendship with Jesus, with others. And it's about joining in with what he is doing in the life of the other person.

- Spend some time thinking about the ways in which your friendship with Jesus already spills over into your relationships.
- Ask him how that might change as you continue to join him on his journey today.
- Ask him if there are specific people he would like to see you growing in friendship with.

Close this prayer time by thanking God for all the people he has brought you into contact with, and for his work in their lives.

Day 4: An open door

During one of my prayer times I found myself taken to the simple image of a door in a seemingly impassable wall. Maybe you could join me there. The wall seems to go on as far as I can see in both directions and it's high, there seems to be no way through. Place yourself there and look at the wall. I've taken many people to this place in prayer and everyone sees a different kind of wall.

As you look more closely you see a door in the wall, and it's slightly ajar. From whatever is on the other side of the wall beautiful light is streaming out through the open door into the space where you are standing.

Jesus is waiting at the door. For some people he is on the outside because they have difficulty entering, for others he is behind the door and they go through to meet him. Go to the door in your imagination and as you meet Jesus, let him take you wherever he wants.

You may find yourself in a landscape, if that's the case look at your surroundings, close by and further afield. Or you may be inside a room or a building. See where Jesus is in this image and what he is doing. He may have things to say to you, or it may be enough just to be with him.

- Allow time for the image to progress. Ask Jesus where he wants to take you.
- Keep going; there may be a number of stages to the journey.
- Keep in step with Jesus.

When you sense the journey is complete, talk to Jesus about what you have experienced, thank him for meeting you. Capture what you have seen, heard and experienced in your journal.

Day 5: Repetition

Review the previous four days and reflect on your feelings about what Jesus has been saying to you, and the way in which you feel connected to him and his journey.

- Reflect on the images of God that you find life-giving.
- Do you experience the 'inner freedom' that God has for you?
- How does your friendship with Jesus spill over into other relationships?
- Did Jesus meet you at the door in the wall?

Day 6: Resting prayer

Each sixth day takes a different approach as explained in Chapter 2. Look back at some of the suggestions set out there and use whatever seems helpful today.

At the centre of everything is the truth that God loves each one of us deeply, wonderfully and unconditionally. So on each Day 6 we will simply stay with and rest in that specific truth. Use the time you have intentionally set aside and just rest in the truth of God's love for you. Let it wash over you, hold you, immerse you.

As a lead in to resting prayer today you could read Psalm 8:3-4:

When I consider your heavens, the work of your fingers, the moon and the stars, which you have set in place, what is mankind that you are mindful of them, human beings that you care for them?

It's good to place our personal experience of God into the bigger picture. I'm hoping that you have been experiencing God's love for you during this Retreat. Hold that knowledge closely and then go back to that image from Week 2 of standing with Jesus looking at the stars and the Milky Way. Just stand there with him, knowing his love for you and seeing his handiwork.

You are here to rest in the presence of Jesus, to be held by him. Make yourself present to him as he is present to you. Relax into his love for you for this short time.

Day 7: Day off!

Have a break and do something different of your choosing. Or you might like to engage with the following as a starting point:

Last week on Day 7 we thought about some of the world's conflict areas. There is another conflict which affects the planet as a whole and all living things. Today we are witnessing what some have described as the 'Sixth Extinction'.[10] As the impact of human activity increases so does the number of species pushed to (and over) the edge of extinction. Climate change is a key part of the problem and its affects are being increasingly felt, especially by the poorest nations.

---

10. Elizabeth Kolbert, *The Sixth Extinction: An Unnatural History* (London: Bloomsbury, 2015).

We know that God is pleased with his creation and that he has never ceased in his creative activity. We share a responsibility for the planet as its stewards. It's easy to become overwhelmed by the scale of this, and other, global challenges. Today bring the things that particularly concern you to Jesus. Ask him to help you take practical steps to engage in his creative care of planet Earth.

Week 7: The Final Stages of the Journey

This week sees the beginning of the most difficult part of the journey. We will take part in the events that led to the cross. A journey that started with high hopes by the River Jordan at Jesus' baptism is now heading towards apparent tragedy. You have come this far with Jesus and his other followers; love and friendship will hold you in the story. You have become part of his journey back then just as you are part of what he is doing today.

Day 1: Entering Jerusalem on a donkey

Read Matthew 21:1-11

Riding into Jerusalem on a donkey symbolises Jesus' vulnerability and the gulf between the kingdom he proclaimed and those of the Roman and Jewish authorities.

Read again verses 6-11 and as you do imagine yourself walking alongside the donkey's head. You could be holding its reins, guiding it through the crowds. With each step you are drawing closer to danger as you enter the city and negotiate its narrow streets.

Take a look around at the crowds, feel the cloaks and palm branches under your feet as you walk forward. Look back towards Jesus sitting on the donkey; what is he doing, how is this welcome affecting him? He knows how the week is going to unfold, you don't.

- Take your time. Donkeys walk quite slowly and there are crowds hemming you in.
- How are you feeling as this journey unfolds?
- Now think about other situations where you have (or are right now) walking in vulnerability.
- What difference does it make to be walking alongside Jesus?

Speak to him in prayer about how you feel about experiencing vulnerability.

As an aside, I wonder if, like me, you prefer certainty to vulnerability? I would not take part in this journey were it not for the friendship I'm sharing. I'm here because I need to be close to my friend.

Day 2: Jesus washing the disciples' feet

Read John 13:1-17

Just a few hours before his crucifixion, Jesus gathered his disciples for a final meal. There are many things he wants to say to them at this last supper together. His washing their feet is a powerful symbol underpinning his words.

Can you allow Jesus to wash your feet? You may find that's more difficult than it is for you to wash the feet of others.

Read the passage again and imagine yourself in the room. It's evening, the meal has been served, and now you see Jesus get up and do the job of a servant. You hear the conversation with Peter and now it's your turn.

It may help to take off whatever you have on your feet as you imagine Jesus kneeling before you.

Presenting your feet can be an act of making yourself vulnerable to his love and also to being served by him.

- Can you allow Jesus to serve you in this way?
- Do you identify with Peter's response – I'm not good enough for you to do this for me, this seems all wrong?
- See the washing of your feet by Jesus as a gift of his friendship, a grace gift to you.

Take your time with this and speak to Jesus about your feelings as he demonstrates love and service in this tangible way.

Day 3: The Garden of Gethsemane

Read Matthew 26:36-46

We have reached another turning point. Matthew records the events of Jesus' last hours before his arrest, and the inability of the disciples to stay awake and keep watch. I wonder if you or I would have fallen asleep as well as the disciples. I want to be there accompanying Jesus whatever the cost, but this could be a struggle.

Read the passage again and imagine yourself there in the garden, waiting for events to unfold. Could you have kept watch? Could I?

When entering this story, I had the sense of Jesus saying:

You are accompanying me... this will be your life. There will be times for you to sit and watch, just be alongside, and similar times when I will do this for you. Times of suffering as well as times of joy, eating together and being part of something new, living and growing. Then times of confinement and attack. In your imagination we have walked from the carpenter's shop to Gethsemane. At certain points all you can do is be present, to sit and wait and if possible, keep awake.

As I write I'm thinking of time spent with a good friend, John, in the final weeks of his life. There was nothing I could do apart from pray and be there with him. While I was doing that I witnessed Jesus coming to him in prayer, preparing him for his death. Jesus was showing John that he was alongside him in this final stage of his journey, and that all the aspects of his life had value and that there were still things they would do together. Those times of prayer with John were unforgettable. I've included that story at the end of this book.

- Think about the times when there was little or nothing you could do, except be present with someone you care about, in the presence of Jesus.
- How did that make you feel?

Are there people you would like to pray for? If so, why not do that now? In your imagination sit with them, with Jesus present, watch and wait.

Day 4: Arrest and trial

Read Matthew 26:47-68

The account of Jesus' arrest and trial recorded in Matthew's Gospel brings lots of questions to the surface. What do you do with your questions? Often I put them to one side, but Jesus seems to welcome them.

Judas travelled with Jesus for three years, witnessed the miracles, and heard his teaching before betraying him. He didn't just leave Jesus, he sought to destroy or manipulate him. Those of us who have followed Jesus for many years – do we also destroy him, unwittingly? Are some expressions of Christianity, in fact, self-destructive?

Faced with the intimidation of the authorities, would you and I have fled with the other disciples?

Jesus' trial was a complete reversal of the way things should have been. His accusers should have been standing before him. Here Peter provides an example of friendship; he could not keep away regardless of the risk. He had to be as close to Jesus as he could be. That's all he could do. But in the end the pressure was too great and he denied the one he loved.

Peter was a friend who could not stay away or be separated. He was also fearful and misguided at times. But see him again in full flow convincing the crowd in Acts 2. His failure does not prevent Jesus working through him in the future.

Jesus is on trial every day, in the media, in conversation.

- Are there times when you don't have the answer, or perhaps one that does not seem to convince?
- How do you feel if you fail to deliver a convincing defence when Jesus is on trial in your presence?
- Why can it be so difficult to explain Jesus to others?

Bring your answers to these questions to Jesus in prayer. Tell him how you feel. Hear what he has to say in reply.

Day 5: Repetition

Review the previous four days and reflect on your feelings about what Jesus has been saying to you, and the way in which you feel connected to him and his journey.

The events covered this week are a foretaste of what is to come as Jesus is crucified.

- How have the last four days affected you?
- Do you sense and have you entered into Jesus' vulnerability?

Day 6: Resting prayer

Each sixth day takes a different approach as explained in Chapter 2. Look back at some of the suggestions set out there and use whatever seems helpful today.

At the centre of everything is the truth that God loves each one of us deeply, wonderfully and unconditionally. So on each Day 6 we will simply stay with that specific truth. Use the time you have intentionally set aside and just rest in the truth of God's love for you. Let it wash over you, hold you, immerse you.

As a lead in to resting prayer today you could read Psalm 18:1-2:

I love you, Lord, my strength. The Lord is my rock, my fortress and my deliverer; my God is my rock, in whom I take refuge ...

You are here to rest in the presence of Jesus, to be held by him. Make yourself present to him as he is present to you. Relax into his love for you for this short time.

Day 7: Day off!

Have a break and do something different of your choosing. Or you might like to engage with the following as a starting point:

Over the last two weeks our Day 7 journey has focused on the conflict zones and challenges faced by our planet. One effect of these challenges has been the displacement of people and whole communities as they seek to escape from war, drought, flood and starvation. Jesus' started life as a refugee as Mary and Joseph fled from Herod immediately after his birth. Maybe you know some asylum seekers or refugees personally or are aware of their needs in your own community and country.

You could today pray for people displaced from home for whatever reason and imagine Jesus right there amongst them. Maybe you could see him on an unseaworthy boat attempting to cross the Mediterranean from North African to Europe, or in a refugee camp. As you pray, ask for him to reach out to all those seeking safety and shelter; and to do that through people such as you and me.

Week 8: The Cross

During this week we will follow Jesus to the cross and the tomb. Entering this part of the story is not easy, but love and friendship continue to draw us close to him and hold us in the story.

Day 1: Jesus is mocked and tormented

Read Matthew 27:27-31 and Luke 22:63-65

Mel Gibson's film *The Passion of the Christ* (2004) brought home the reality of a Roman scourging. The flogging scene is brutal. Matthew and Luke did not need to describe this event; their readers knew exactly what would have happened. Imagine yourself as a witness.

I would have hated seeing this; it would have been devastating. Yet many of Jesus' followers today are going through the same kind of experience. Can my horror and outrage at the treatment Jesus received be expressed in some positive way towards those being persecuted today? How does he regard those who are sharing in his suffering?

During my conversation with Jesus as I read Matthew's account I sensed him speaking to me about the cost of following him. Leaving the security of our 'carpenter's workshop' is a starting point, but as we confront the powers that seek to run this world, the cost becomes greater, ever greater.

When Jesus was tempted after his baptism his identity was challenged, but he knew who he was and lived from that truth. Now as he approached the cross the circumstances shouted out that he was living an illusion and that he had failed. But the truth had never changed; he was always loved by the Father, was full of the Holy Spirit, and was true to his purpose.

Reflecting on this passage I experienced Jesus speaking directly to confront the most basic assumptions that underpin the way I see myself and live my life.

This event is a strong example of what it means to live in the truth and not in a lie. Whatever your circumstances, live in the truth – that you are deeply and wonderfully loved and that I am always your friend. The circumstances make no difference to the truth, as you can see from what happened to me.

Neglecting to live as a deeply and wonderfully loved person, whatever the circumstances, is to live a lie. But it's the way I often see things.

I need time to let this soak in. I also need to return to this place again and again.

- Reflect on your circumstances, your trials and the things that cause you pain.
- Can you hold on to the fact that you are deeply and wonderfully loved?
- How does that change things?

Speak to Jesus to thank him for the trials he went through because of his love for you.

Day 2: Carrying the cross

Read Mark 15:21 and Luke 23:26

We don't know much about Simon, other than that his home town/region was Cyrene (probably in what is now Libya). The Gospel writers add some personal details: that he was coming in from the country and his sons were called Rufus and Alexander. Some commentators think this family became believers and were therefore known to the Gospel writers, hence their interest in these details.

Simon carried something for Jesus, something heavy and hard to bear. He had no choice in the matter; he was a victim of other people's choice and will. Take a moment to think what it was like for Simon, the crowds, the atmosphere of violent intent, the intimidating Roman soldiers. Try to walk some of that journey in your imagination and focus on your experience and feelings – the pain, exhaustion, fear…

We don't know if there was any interaction between Simon and Jesus. If there had been, what do you think Jesus would have said to Simon? If Jesus gave Simon eye contact, what would that have been like?

Now think about the things you are carrying for Jesus; some may bring joy, others may be heavy burdens. What is it like for you to be carrying something for Jesus?

- What is Jesus saying to you as you carry things for him?
- Is he thanking you, or asking you to be patient? Maybe he is asking you to keep pace with him – not falling behind or rushing ahead?
- Is it difficult to hear and receive what he is saying to you?

Speak to Jesus about the things you carry for him, hear what he has to say in reply.

Day 3: The crucifixion

Read John 19:17-30

This is a terrible place; there are crowds of onlookers, soldiers, people mocking and shouting abuse. In amongst all of that is a small group of Jesus' followers, his mother and her sister, Mary the wife of Clopas, Mary Magdalene and John. You might like to imagine yourself standing with this small group watching and listening. There is nothing you can do to influence the outcome of this story, all you can do is watch and wait. Being at the cross and watching Jesus die is shocking but love and friendship hold you there; you cannot walk away.

Even on the cross Jesus reaches out to others. You hear him making sure his mother is cared for, and giving an assurance to one of those being crucified next to him. He exclaims that what he came to do is now complete. He is there for you and me.

Read the passage in John again, and if you have time, the other Gospel accounts.

- Imagining yourself there, hear again Jesus' words from the cross.
- See if he has something to say to you from that place.
- Be open to wherever he takes you, it could be a surprising journey.

Saying thank you seems inadequate, but do that in your own way in the light of your experience at the cross.

Day 4: The Tomb

Read Luke 23:50-56

Where was Jesus between his burial and resurrection? Does his experience have parallels in your life and mine?

At Easter we focus on Jesus' crucifixion and resurrection, but the time in-between also seems important. It speaks to me about things that have come to an end, and times of rest before moving on to whatever is next. I can see the value of building such pauses into my life.

The tomb was a dark, silent, lonely place, but it was also a place of peace and preparation. In thinking about the significance of that day I sensed Jesus speaking to me about things in my life that I need to die to and leave behind in the tomb.

At this point in the Ignatian Spiritual Exercises I reflected on the times when I feel anxious and fearful and my need to be in control. Not things you can deal with once and for all. But things I would like to put in the tomb and leave behind.

The image of the tomb is powerful and in an unexpected way, life-giving. It's a place to leave things behind and move on. It's also a place to return to from time to time.

- Speak to Jesus about the things you wish to lay in the tomb.
- It may help if you write them down on slips of paper and then place them in a box.
- Imagine rolling a stone across the tomb entrance and walking away.

Ask Jesus to come alongside as you enter into and then walk away from the tomb.

Day 5: Repetition

Review the previous four days and reflect on your feelings about what Jesus has been saying to you, and the way in which you feel connected to him and his journey.

Think again about:

- The things you are carrying.
- Being present with Jesus at the cross.
- Laying things down in the tomb.

In prayer thank Jesus for being with you in all the seasons of your life, including those times that feel like being in a tomb.

Day 6: Resting prayer

Each sixth day takes a different approach as explained in Chapter 2. Look back at some of the suggestions set out there and use whatever seems helpful today.

At the centre of everything is the truth that God loves each one of us deeply, wonderfully and unconditionally. So on each Day 6 we rest in that specific truth. Use the time you have intentionally set aside and just rest in the truth of God's love for you. Let it wash over you, hold you, immerse you.

Today you could take a lead into your time of resting prayer from the story of the sisters Martha and Mary. We met them briefly in the story of Lazarus in Week 5. Luke 10:38-42 tells us about another visit to the home of Lazarus and his sisters when Martha was distracted by all her responsibilities while Mary sat at Jesus' feet.

'Martha, Martha,' the Lord answered, 'you are worried and upset about many things, but few things are needed – or indeed only one. Mary has chosen what is better, and it will not be taken away from her.'

Take your lead from Mary today and imagine yourself sitting at his feet, the one thing that is needed.

You are here to rest in the presence of Jesus, to be held by him. Make yourself present to him as he is present to you. Relax into his love for you for this short time.

Day 7: Day off!

Have a break and do something different of your choosing. Or you might like to engage with the following as a starting point:

The last three reflections for Day 7 have taken us into hard places. Now, as a way of concluding these meditations, my suggestion is to look forward. Firstly into God's big picture for 'new creation' and then into those things that bring hope into your own situation.

Revelation 21:1-4 describes new creation, a place and a time when God will put all things right:

Then I saw 'a new heaven and a new earth', for the first heaven and the first earth had passed away, and there was no longer any sea. I saw the Holy City, the new Jerusalem, coming down out of heaven from God, prepared as a bride beautifully dressed for her husband. And I heard a loud voice from the throne saying, 'Look! God's dwelling-place is now among the people, and he will dwell with them. They will be his people, and God himself will be with them and be their God. "He will wipe every tear from their eyes. There will be no more death" or mourning or crying or pain, for the old order of things has passed away.'

This rich image follows on well from our journey to the cross this week, and the anticipation of Jesus' resurrection. Take some time today to let God take you into his future as described by John.

Week 9: Resurrection

After the horror leading up to the death and burial of Jesus, this week we witness the events that will take us forward into our own experience of Jesus and his journey today.

Day 1: Resurrection

Read Matthew 28:1-10

Last week our journey with Jesus concluded at the tomb. A dark, silent, lonely place, but also a place of peace and preparation. Today we will enter the garden with the two Marys, the first of Jesus' followers to meet the risen Lord.

Take a few moments to imagine what the Marys were thinking and talking about as they went to 'look at the tomb'. Did they have any expectation about what was just going to happen? They were carrying with them the sights and sounds of crucifixion.

Now join the Marys as they cross the garden and witness the events described by Matthew – an earthquake, an angel who rolled back the stone and then sat on it! More than enough to stop you in your tracks!

Hear for yourself the words of the angel: 'Do not be afraid, for I know that you are looking for Jesus, who was crucified. He is not here: he has risen, just as he said. Come and see the place where he lay. Then go quickly and tell his disciples: "He has risen from the dead and is going ahead of you into Galilee…"' How were these words spoken? How did they affect the Marys? How are they affecting you?

You take up the angel's invitation to look inside the tomb. Imagine doing that, feel the cool air inside the tomb… you see the rough-hewn walls, but where is the body?

With the two Marys you set out quickly to tell the other disciples, but then watch as they meet Jesus himself. Listen to their conversation, they are overcome with emotion.

Matthew does not tell us how long the two women stayed with Jesus in the garden before hurrying away.

- Imagine yourself lingering there for a while after the women have gone.
- Just you in the garden with the risen Jesus, what would that be like?
- What would you say to him, what might he say to you?

Capture in your journal what you have experienced and any words or impressions you receive from Jesus.

Day 2: The road to Emmaus

Read Luke 24:13-35

It's the first Easter Sunday – resurrection day, the greatest day in history. Imagine that you are walking with two friends from Jerusalem to Emmaus; for you this is not a day of rejoicing but one of confusion and disappointment.

It's a 11km (7 mile) walk, maybe three hours or so on the road, but you are in no mood to hurry. It's the afternoon and hot. Passover has ended and there are others making the same journey on a normal working day. There is plenty to see on the road, animals being driven, carts and mules, people at the roadside trading and begging. It's noisy and smelly at times; the dust and flies are a nuisance.

You feel totally weary and it's not because of the journey. You and your friends are confused and downcast. Over the last three years you have invested so much in Jesus, travelling with him, seeing his miracles, loving his teaching. For you he was the hope for Israel's future, and now those hopes have been dashed. Jesus is dead and buried. You are also confused by some reports you heard before setting out, that some of the women had seen him alive.

As you come alongside the two disciples in your imagination, reflect on your own personal disappointments and confusion about Jesus. Why was my friend not healed? Why did that relationship fail? Why does God seem so distant? Why doesn't he guide me in this important decision? You've invested so much in your relationship with Jesus, but there are so many unanswered questions.

Back on the road, a stranger joins you; he is not downcast at all. You think him to be foolish and ignorant – how could he not know about what has happened in Jerusalem over the last three days? You tell him what you are feeling and he starts to talk to the three of you.

You and your friends are the foolish ones and ignorant! He takes you on a journey through the Scriptures to show that all that happened to Jesus was necessary and prophesied.

Now he turns to you and asks you how things are with you.

- What are your hopes and fears?
- What do you say to him and what does he say in return?
- How do you feel in his presence?
- Are you beginning to see things in a new light and experience the kind of hope that you haven't had for a long time?

You reach a crossroads and the stranger has his own journey to make.

- How would it feel if you separated now?
- You share a meal with him and as he passes you a piece of bread you realise who he is.

Talk to him about your hopes and fears and then reach out your hand over the table to receive the bread from him.

Day 3: Jesus welcomes our questions

Read John 20:24-30

Thomas witnessed Jesus' miracles, heard his teaching, and was drawn into his friendship. He was at the heart of things. That didn't stop him asking questions or making bold statements. In John 11:16 when the news came to Jesus of Lazarus' death, Thomas says to the other disciples, 'Let us also go, that we may die with him.' Later in John 14:5 when Jesus is talking about his death and leaving the disciples it's Thomas who comes in with the question: 'Lord, we don't know where you are going, so how can we know the way?'

I don't think Thomas was any more doubting than the other disciples – it's just that he was the one bold enough to say what he was thinking.

What was Jesus' response to Thomas? He did not rebuke Thomas for his doubts. Instead he invited him to see the evidence for himself: 'See my hands and side, if you need to do this, examine my wounds.' Those words from Jesus – how were they spoken? 'Stop doubting and believe.' I would like to think said with a smile on Jesus' face: 'Come on, Thomas, it's really me.' Thomas' answer is immediate: 'My Lord and my God!' No record of this but I can see Jesus embracing Thomas after this exchange and lots of weeping and laughter in the room.

Thomas is a great role model for our journey into friendship with Jesus.

How do churches handle their Thomases? Often not well. They can be seen as threatening or undermining. Or they can be listened to and helped to walk through periods of doubt and uncertainty for as long as that takes.

We can help those with doubts and questions in the same way

that Jesus dealt with Thomas. Jesus asked Thomas to confront the evidence and his doubts together. And only then did he invite Thomas to believe.

Read again the account and then enter the story described by John, imagining yourself as Thomas. You have questions and are perhaps out of sync with your friends who seem to have all the answers.

- How do you feel – a bit isolated, defensive?
- Jesus picks up on the things that concern you, the things that just don't make sense.
- Jesus already knows what those things are, so why not speak to him about them now? Be open, don't hold back.

You hold no surprises for him. Now take some time to listen to Jesus, hear what he has to say to you. Is he showing you something that will take you a step further on your journey?

Day 4: Reinstatement and commissioning

Read John 21:1-19

The disciples have gone back to a familiar place, their Galilee; join them in the fishing boat in your imagination as you read John's account.

It's beginning to get light as you head back to the shore. As you come closer in you can see a lone figure standing on the beach tending a fire and looking out in your direction. It's not light enough to see who it is but you can just catch the smell of fish being cooked on the fire; he's been more successful than you have.

The boat comes into shore and the stranger calls out asking if you've caught anything. Your friends answer no. Then he says, 'Throw your net on the right side ... and you will find some' (John 21:6). In the rush to pull in the nets the stranger is forgotten, until you hear John shout out, 'It's the Lord, it's Jesus!' Peter the fisherman loses interest in the fish in his eagerness to join Jesus, he's first into the water and ashore as the rest of you struggle to keep the boat afloat and bring in the catch.

Finally, you too are on the beach wading through the cool water, feeling the sand under your feet as with the others you race up the beach towards Jesus.

You feel elated, so pleased to be with Jesus again. You gather together around the fire and Jesus shares with you some bread and some fish. You feel secure in his presence; you have so many questions, but right now just being with him is enough.

Jesus takes Peter to one side and talks to him. You can hear the conversation. 'Do you love me?' Three times the same question and then a fresh commissioning: 'Take care of my sheep.'

Now Jesus turns to you and draws you into conversation.

- Like Peter, can you think of times of denial when you have let him down?
- Hear Jesus asking you the same question: 'Do you love me?'
- What do you say and what does Jesus say in reply?

Use your journal to turn these questions into a conversation with Jesus.

Day 5: Repetition

Both the angel and Jesus instruct the disciples to go to Galilee to meet him there. Do you have a 'Galilee', a familiar place where meeting Jesus for the friendship of conversation seems natural? It could be a particular seat in the place where you live, or in the open in a park or on a beach. It may be a few moments of quiet you can snatch anywhere in the busyness of your day. Go there either physically or in your imagination and meet with Jesus who has already gone ahead of you and is waiting to greet you.

Review the previous four days and reflect on your feelings about what Jesus has been saying to you, and the way in which you feel connected to him and his journey.

- Did you meet Jesus in the garden after his resurrection?
- Or on the road to Emmaus?
- Can you bring your questions and doubts to him?
- Do you have a Galilee?

Day 6: Resting prayer

Each sixth day takes a different approach as explained in Chapter 2. Look back at some of the suggestions set out there and use whatever seems helpful today.

At the centre of everything is the truth that God loves each one of us deeply, wonderfully and unconditionally. So on each Day 6 we will simply stay with that specific truth. Use the time you have intentionally set aside and just rest in the truth of God's love for you. Let it wash over you, hold you, immerse you.

Today you might like to read Mark 10:13-16 which tells how Jesus welcomed little children and encourages us to adopt a childlike faith.

Let the little children come to me, and do not hinder them, for the kingdom of God belongs to such as these. Truly I tell you, anyone who will not receive the kingdom of God as a little child will never enter it.' And he took the children in his arms, placed his hands on them and blessed them.

Read again Miye's story of her encounter with Jesus on the beach in the Introduction, experienced during a time of resting prayer.

You are here to rest in the presence of Jesus, to be held by him. Make yourself present to him as he is present to you. Relax into his love for you for this short time.

Day 7: Day off!

Have a break and do something different of your choosing. Or you might like to engage with the following as a starting point:

It may be good to focus again on your own situation, starting with the people who are part of your life – your family, neighbours, friends and work colleagues. You could use the time you have today to bring them in prayer to Jesus, asking him how you can best join in with the things he is doing in their lives.

Week 10: New Beginnings

The Ascension of Jesus marks the end of one story and the beginning of another. That was true for the disciples and also for you and me. Accompanying Jesus in the Gospel story draws us into his friendship and that continues as he is present with us today by his Spirit.

Now at this point of transition marked in Acts by the Ascension and the coming of the Spirit, we continue our journey engaging with what Jesus is doing here and now, in the only time we have – the present moment.

Day 1: Ascension

Read Acts 1:1-11

Imagine yourself present listening to Jesus as he speaks to the disciples. Watch as he disappears from your sight. How do you feel now he is no longer physically with you?

Remember that he is now more present in the world than when he lived here as a man.

- Think about some of your own big transitions. How did you feel? What was it like moving forward into something new?
- Think about transitions that may be coming up. They could be related to your work, health, family contexts.
- As you approach change, who and what is it that guides you and sets your compass? What is it that energises you and gives life?

Bring these questions to Jesus in conversation.

Day 2: The Spirit

Read Acts 2:1-13

Jesus was no longer physically with the disciples but now he is present by the Holy Spirit. The Spirit that flowed through Jesus' life, that same Spirit is given to his followers.

It's interesting to review different expressions of the work of the Holy Spirit in the recent past. You may have a particular take on, say, the Pentecostal movement at the beginning of the twentieth century, the charismatic movement of the 1970s, or the 'Toronto Blessing' of the 1990s. Then there are quite different moves of the

Spirit, as churches have engaged with the poor and social justice. And where does new monasticism and Taizé fit into this picture?

We tend to focus on our particular experience of the Spirit, and can be resistant to other expressions. Can you go wider than your own particular background and 'tribal group'? I think we are called to be true to Scripture and open to the diversity of what Jesus is doing.

Take some time to think about your own experience of the Holy Spirit.

- How aware are you of the work of the Spirit within you at the present time?
- Ask Jesus what receiving more of his Spirit could mean for you.
- Tell him what you desire.

Speak to him now and see what he says in reply.

Day 3: Freeing God to be who he is

Back in Week 6, Day 2 we explored the theme of 'inner freedom', being able to let go of loved people and possessions. I described drawing up a list and invited you to do the same.

Doing this a few years ago opened up a wider conversation during which I discovered that Jesus was thinking about something else – the way I seek to own and control him, and shape him to my own ends. To my surprise our conversation went like this:

Adrian: It's helpful to see that being free is to release others to be who they are, and by so doing provide a way for them to return love to us. This seems to be an illustration of the way in which you love.

Jesus: You do not own me. Some people think they do and manipulate who they think I am for their own purposes. Give up any lingering ideas you may have about owning me or any aspect of my kingdom. Not owning me sets you free to be who you are and who I want you to truly be. When you 'set me free' to be who I am rather than being a prisoner of your imagining, when you give up your 'ownership', you will discover more fully who I am.

What I found shocking about this exchange was the realisation that I tend to put God in a box of my own making, I keep him 'safe' enough for me to handle. I do this unconsciously.

One of the ways in which I limit God is in my perception of his love for me. Most of the time I simply do not believe he loves me in the way he says he does – either in Scripture or in those moments of closeness when I'm personally conscious of his affirmation. Do you have the same problem – does God's love for you seem just too much?

- Spend some time reflecting on whether you keep God safe rather than allowing him to be who he really is.
- Ask him to show you how you can allow him to love you the way he wants to.

This is such an important area to explore; it will take time and perhaps today simply opens an ongoing conversation.

Day 4: Joining Jesus on his journey today

Joining Jesus in the Gospel story can help us to connect to him in a new way. This is less about concepts and more about experiencing friendship. If you have come this far, I'm hoping that has been your experience. Often when we meet Jesus in a specific story he takes us somewhere else and shows how he is already present in what we think of as our story.

I'm aware that my 'standard' model for living is one that places me at the centre of things. Yes, I am seeking to follow Jesus in all aspects of my life, asking for his guidance and help as I attempt this. And that is the point, this is my journey and I'm asking Jesus to join me. Even in a context of reliance and trust I still naturally default back to starting with myself, my current issues, challenges and opportunities, and seek God's help to get through all of that. But is that so bad?

During the Ignatian Spiritual Exercises I began to see that there is another way of looking at things – that I can join Jesus on his journey rather than asking him to join me on mine. I feel that he invites me to do so. This feels like a radical shift, and one not easily accomplished. My default settings are hardwired within me, it is taking time for a new approach to become so well-established that the old fades away through disuse.

Look at the Gospel story – who invited who? The first disciples did not invite Jesus to share their journey; that is a ridiculous idea. Without him their lives would have been unremarkable and we would never have heard of them, former fishermen, tax collectors, and prostitutes, priests and family members; people living in an unimportant country on the edge of the Roman Empire. Joining Jesus on his journey changed everything for them, as it does for us today.

Easy to see when we look at Jesus' followers during his time on the earth; but for you and I today, how might this work out?

One of the pivotal moments in the Exercises came as I spent time at the foot of the cross. I had the sense of Jesus giving me a word from the cross, something particularly important I needed to respond to. And yet it came in an everyday package I could readily relate to. I'm going to set it out in more detail than I would normally:

In my imagination I'm driving my car on the M6 motorway and stop at a service station I know well. While sitting in the café enjoying a coffee break, I'm joined at my table by someone strangely familiar who engages me in conversation. After a while he points out that my conventional way of travelling around illustrates how I live as a Christian – in charge of what I'm doing, with my own map and agenda to guide me, stopping once in a while to recharge, sometimes seeking directions and help, and then off again.

Having gently pointed this out he makes me an intriguing offer – rather than me carrying on driving, why don't I join him on the train? As it happens a rail line runs right next to the M6 at this particular service station.

It's an attractive idea – relaxing in conversation with my new friend, no need to stop to refuel, a buffet car for refreshment, and an opportunity to share with him the view from the window. I hesitate; giving up the steering wheel goes against the grain, I like to be in control, but I'm warming so much to my new companion that I agree.

Now we are sitting together on the train in a group of four seats around a table. He already has a seat marked with my name on it opposite him. As we look out of the window, he explains that I will begin to see things as he sees them – some of the views will be beautiful and inspiring, some will be devastating and deeply distressing, but whatever comes into view we will be together.

From time to time we are joined by others at our table, but strangely during our conversation they don't see my companion, although I'm still aware of his presence.

Then we take a walk down the carriage, stopping every so often to talk with others. Sometimes my companion takes the lead in the conversation and I listen and watch what is happening. Other times we reverse roles and I take the lead and my companion watches what I'm doing and saying.

Occasionally we enter another carriage with a completely different group of people and again we take turns in leading the conversation.

Always we come back to our original seats and compare notes on the things we have heard and the people we have met. We look at the views from the window and reflect on them. There's always time to relax and enjoy the day and each other's company. Being together and sharing friendship is the most important part of the journey.

The point behind the image is nothing to do with trains and cars but everything to do with who owns the journey.

- Like me, are you unsure about what throwing away your car keys and joining Jesus on his journey might mean, or how that could work in practice?
- How do you feel about joining Jesus on his journey rather than asking him to help you on yours?
- What would be your way of expressing the idea of joining Jesus 'on the train'?

Engaging with these questions may mark the opening of an ongoing conversation with Jesus.

Day 5: Repetition

Review the previous four days and reflect on your feelings about what Jesus has been saying to you, and the way in which you feel connected to him and his journey.

- Reflect on transitions you have faced in the past and any that are coming up, and how they are part of your journey with Jesus.
- Can you 'allow' God to be who he really is?
- What would be your expression of throwing away your car keys and joining Jesus?

Day 6: Resting Prayer

Each sixth day takes a different approach as explained in Chapter 2. Look back at some of the suggestions set out there and use whatever seems helpful today.

At the centre of everything is the truth that God loves each one of us deeply, wonderfully and unconditionally. So on each Day 6 we will simply stay with that specific truth. Use the time you have intentionally set aside and just rest in the truth of God's love for you. Let it wash over you, hold you, immerse you.

Let's return to the starting point back in Week 1, using this prayer from the *Iona Abbey Worship Book: Service of Quiet* to lead in to resting prayer.

You might like to imagine yourself in a quiet place of worship that you are familiar with, in company with others, or alone, entering God's presence.

Jesus, you commanded waves to be still and calmed a stormy sea. Quieten now my restless heart that I may find rest in you. I recognise the noises inside me and the noises around me. I acknowledge them, but seek here to know your presence in the midst of all that might distract me. So, now, I surrender for these moments my speech, knowing that beneath the silence is a deeper Word, and even when I say nothing, you are still listening.

Ever listening, ever watchful, ever loving God, I rest in you.[11]

---

11. The Iona Community, *Iona Abbey Worship Book*. (See pages 53-54.) Adapted for personal use.

You are here to rest in the presence of Jesus, to be held by him. Make yourself present to him as he is present to you. Relax into his love for you for this short time.

Day 7: Day off!

Have a break and do something different of your choosing. Or you might like to engage with the following as a starting point:

Our Day 7 journey has taken us far and wide. Now at the end of this Retreat, why not return to the place where you started, the place where you live – physically and spiritually.

Go around the room(s) of the place where you live and imagine Jesus there with you.

When you have done that, return to where you have chosen to pray and invite him into the 'rooms' of your personal life. If you can, tell him there are no hidden corners that are out of bounds for him.

- How does it feel to give Jesus unfettered access to every part of your life?
- Speak to him about your feelings and capture the conversation in your journal.

Finally, reflect on the difference between the first time you prayed in this way and how it feels now.

- Has your relationship with Jesus has changed on this journey?

You have reached the end of one stage and the beginning of another.

3. Conclusion: A Sense of Homecoming

Friendship with Jesus at the heart of your journey

A number of years ago I visited Ephesus with a couple of friends. It was exciting to be walking streets trodden by Paul, reflecting on the impact he made there and the trouble that landed him in! Our visit included a little publicised site – the tomb of St John. To one side of the main Ephesus tourist sites are the remains of an ancient church. There are just a few walls left of what must once have been a substantial building.

Four simple columns, and at that time a gated-off stairway leading down into a crypt, with a small plaque stating 'The tomb of St John' written only in English. It was the most understated 'monument' I have ever seen, yet to me it seemed perfect, a place where you could sit and reflect without any distraction.

It was early in the morning and there were no other visitors, so we paused to share bread and a drink together and remember Jesus. As we did so I had an overwhelming sense of the presence of Jesus with us, no sense of the presence of John, just Jesus. We prayed, giving thanks for the bread we were about to share. As we did, three white butterflies appeared and hovered around the bread before flying away again. The presence of Jesus and an image of the Trinity, the power of that experience remains with me to this day.

Jesus sought to draw each of the disciples into his friendship, as he does today. John is referred to as the disciple 'Jesus loved' (see John 13:23; 19:26; 20:2; 21:7,20). I don't think that was to say that John was in some way more loved than the others. Rather it was to show Jesus' intention for each of us. I'm not sure exactly what was happening on that morning in Ephesus, but I do know that Jesus loved John, and at that place and time God chose to make his presence, love and friendship known to us as well, in a powerful and intimate way.

I'm coming to realise more and more that friendship is the overarching quality of our relationship with Jesus. Other aspects of that relationship are lived out within the context of friendship, including serving and discipleship. That friendship is not remote and occasional, but warm, encouraging, challenging and available to us every day.

There are things each of us can do which will help that friendship deepen and grow. It's about conversation, listening, doing and seeing things together, serving, sitting at table eating together, sharing his joy and his sorrow as we see things as he sees them.

It's about widening the ways in which we pray. We can experience truth as we allow the Holy Spirit to guide our imagination. We can capture what we experience by journaling our impressions and those conversations with Jesus. And later we can read again, revisit and enjoy a deepening of that most important friendship.

The place you live from

This is the place I want to live from, sharing Jesus' journey today in close friendship. Seeing the things he sees, the beautiful and the ugly, engaged in what he is doing, sharing some of the cost of all of that.

I opened this book with a description of crossing a short stretch of water on the ferry with Jesus. We were travelling together to an island that represented the day ahead. We shared the journey talking about the people, places and events we were likely to encounter. The ten-minute crossing set up the day, and the journey home provided the same space for reflection and anticipation.

As you have progressed through this short book, I hope that like me you have encountered Jesus and walked some of his journey through the Gospel story. There may have been particularly striking moments when he seemed close and other times when the journey seemed like hard work.

Travelling with Jesus is always at his invitation. He is the one who draws us into what he is doing and into his friendship. That invitation is always open.

Living from a place of friendship with Jesus opens up new possibilities. As that place enlarges, we have more and more room for others, whoever they may be.

Joining Jesus on his journey, seeing things as he does, can be hard and inspiring at the same time. Does it require more or less faith? I'm no longer trying to make things happen myself. It really has to be him, and that's what makes this so exciting.

Each person's experience of friendship is unique. So why have I unpacked what has come out of my particular journey? I've written this book to encourage you to make your own journey. To open your door to Jesus, whatever that means for you. Develop your own conversations with him, over the weeks, and months. And join him on his journey over the years ahead. I don't know where it will take you, but I do know you will not be disappointed.

Iona Abbey – Drawn by Richard Farnell

A final reflection: John's last journey

At the beginning of 2017 a close friend, John, asked me to pray with him as he entered the final weeks of his life. I had known John for more than twenty years, along with his wife, Gill, and their three children. We were good friends with many common interests. John had cancer which was spreading rapidly, he knew his time was limited. He wanted to pray but the effects of his illness and the treatment he was receiving were making it hard for him to focus his thoughts.

As we prayed together I took him in his imagination to a doorway in an otherwise impenetrable wall. (We went there in Week 6, Day 4.) The door was slightly ajar and beautiful afternoon summer sunshine was spilling out into the space where John was standing. I suggested that Jesus was standing on the other side of the door waiting to meet him. Then I waited in silence to see what would happen as John went through the door. This is how he described what happened:

John's first steps through the door led him into a small room where there were comfortable chairs. Jesus was there waiting to meet him. Then he progressed into what he described as a 'cathedral-like space'. Over the next few minutes John looked around the 'space' and described to me what he saw on its' four walls. One wall was covered with all the people he knew from the past and present. The other walls represented different aspects of John's life, interests and passions. At the centre of the 'cathedral' was some kind of work-bench and John saw himself standing there alongside Jesus, they were working on a project together.

John returned to his sitting room surprised by what he had experienced and captured what he had seen in his journal. We talked about it together then and later. It seemed to me that Jesus had graciously surrounded John by images of his life, the things and the people he loved and valued. At the centre of everything John was working on a project with Jesus; it wasn't finished, there was still more to come.

In the coming weeks John had further impressions of Jesus standing alongside him as he faced the reality of what was happening. About ten days before he died, John said that Jesus had spoken to him saying, 'Everything is ready; I'm just waiting for you.' Along with many others I'm still grieving the loss of my friend John.

What was happening during John's final illness? As well as receiving excellent medical care, many people were praying for healing, within the family of City Church in Newcastle, and more widely. In our love for John we cried out to Jesus to heal him, to give him more time. That prayer continued right up to the end. Although John was not healed, something else was happening in his relationship with Jesus.

As we prayed together during those final weeks, I witnessed Jesus showing John something very precious – that they had always been, and were still, travelling together. John's journey through life held Jesus at the very centre and now at the end they were walking through those final days, still together.

Looking back, I can see how John 'experienced truth' through prayer during his final journey.

Appendix: Further Resources

Coming to the end of a course or programme can be difficult. At the end of my nine-month journey through the Ignatian Spiritual Exercises I remember being very uncertain about the direction of my future prayer times. One ongoing benefit of those nine months was the structure they provided. It's something I can continue to use which includes times of reading and meditating on a biblical passage, reflection, conversation and journaling.

Here are a few further resources and suggestions that you might find helpful.

Lectio Divina

This is another form of meditation and prayer with a long history, extending back to St Benedict in the fifth century. There are four simple steps to Lectio: first read, then meditate, thirdly pray and finally act. I have used this way of praying personally and in small groups and found it to be very rewarding.

The key seems to be in slowing down, by allowing sufficient time to savour the text you are reading, pausing when you encounter a word or phrase that is particularly meaningful. Stay with that part of the text for as long as it continues to speak to you.

As you hold the text and meditate on it take note of your feelings, how it is affecting you. For example, in reading Psalm 23 about the Lord leading you through 'green pastures' (verse 2) you could stay there for a while reflecting on the times in your life when God has been particularly close and your experience of him has been restful and rich. You could focus on how that affected you at the time and how you feel in the moment as you look back.

Equally important is to allow God to highlight words and phrases that you react against, such as walking through 'the valley of the shadow of death' (verse 4, NKJV). Rather than avoid images that give rise to fear and negative emotions, take your time and ask yourself why you are feeling this way.

Collect your thoughts, turn them into prayer and see if there is something that God is directing you towards doing.

It's important to take time and careful note of how the passage is affecting you. The Psalms are a particularly rich starting point for practising this form of prayer and meditation. This way of meditating and praying can be used in a group setting which has the additional benefit of being able to share insights and reactions together and pray for one another.

There are many resources to help you engage in this form of prayer. If you want a helpful summary, I recommend Tony Jones, *The Sacred Way: Spiritual Practices for Everyday Life.*[12]

The Examen

In my Foreword I described the idea of making a short ferry crossing between two islands as a way of taking me into each new day. I seek to imagine Jesus with me, and make myself present to him before stepping ashore. Taking the ferry back again at the end of the day can be equally helpful, allowing you to review your day in his presence. (By the way, this doesn't have to take place on a ferry; think about what kind of image would work best for you.)

---

12. Tony Jones, *The Sacred Way: Spiritual Practices for Everyday Life* (Grand Rapids, MI: Zondervan, 2005). (See pages 47-55).

Ignatius encouraged using a prayer of Examen at the end of each day. There are many descriptions of how to structure this kind of prayer. The book by Tony Jones I have just referenced, *The Sacred Way: Spiritual Practices for Everyday Life*, is a good starting point.

One purpose of the Examen is to help you identify the things which draw you towards God and those that have the opposite effect. We thought about that in Week 1, Day 2 in respect of your faith journey so far. The Examen provides an opportunity to undertake a mini-review in relation to the day just spent.

There are five main steps you can progress through when reviewing your day:

1. Consider with gratitude all the good things you have experienced.
2. Identify those times when you were aware of God's presence, together with any challenges he was placing before you, and how you responded.
3. Identify the things you regret doing, thinking or saying.
4. Seek God's forgiveness and consider whether you need to ask others for their forgiveness as well.
5. Look ahead to the coming day asking for God's help as you walk through its challenges.

I would add to that final point: ask Jesus to draw you more closely into whatever he is doing amongst the people and situations you will encounter during the coming day.

As you engage with these steps you may find that one or two of them have particular significance, if that's the case stay there and let God speak further. It's also helpful to focus on your feelings as you review the day and how its events have affected you.

Taking these steps in prayer helps to show how God is engaged in every part of life, the mundane and the inspiring. It also puts you in touch with what was happening inside you and provides an opportunity to take all of that back to God.

Spiritual Direction

I've included a very brief description covering Spiritual Direction, or companionship in Chapter 2. For those wanting to explore this further, a good starting point would be the Retreat Association website: www.retreats.org.uk. The Retreats Association has published Spiritual Direction Guidelines which give an introduction to this ministry. The association also offers a starting point for those seeking a 'director'.

In addition I am aware that the Church of England, and some centres that provide training in spiritual direction, can signpost those seeking this ministry to those who are trained to provide it.

Pray as You Go app

This is a free app you can download onto your phone or tablet. It's produced by 'Jesuit Media Initiatives' and provides a daily call to worship, a reading and an invitation to take part in Imaginative Prayer. Each daily programme lasts about ten to twelve minutes and can be easily included in your daily routine. It's something I often use to help start my day. https://pray-as-you-go.org/

Further Reading

What follows is not a comprehensive reading list, but rather those books that I've found particularly helpful on my journey.

Kevin O'Brien, *The Ignatian Adventure* (Chicago, IL: Loyola Press, 2011)
When I completed the Exercises I worked through this book and found it helpful. I would recommend it to anyone interested in engaging with the Exercises.

Gregory A. Boyd, *Seeing is Believing: Experience Jesus Through Imaginative Prayer* (Grand Rapids, MI: Baker Books, 2004)
There seem to be relatively few books dealing with Imaginative Prayer. One that I have found to be particularly helpful is this one by Gregory Boyd. It provides a biblically and historically grounded explanation of this form of prayer. It also explains the reasons why it is relatively unknown and unpractised in large sections of the Church. I found it both affirming and inspiring.

Margaret Silf, *Landmarks: An Ignatian Journey* (London: DLT, 1998)
Margaret Silf has written many books that can take you further on your journey into Jesus' friendship. In particular I found *Landmarks* to be personally very significant and I know of many others who share that experience.

Helen Cepero, *Journaling as a Spiritual Practice: Encountering God through Attentive Writing* (Downers Grove, IL: InterVarsity Press 2008)
As well as introducing 'dialogue journaling' (which I have entitled 'conversational journaling'), this book also describes other forms of journaling and the 'compass exercise'. People I accompany

have found this helpful in understanding where they are on their journey and discovering ways forward.

Tony Jones, *The Sacred Way: Spiritual Practices for Everyday Life* (Grand Rapids, MI: Zondervan 2005)
This book provides a helpful overview and introduction to a range of spiritual practices including those referred to here.

Dallas Willard, *Hearing God: Developing a Conversational Relationship with God* (Downers Grove IL: InterVarsity Press, 2012)
This provides some rich insights into hearing God's voice clearly and developing an intimate relationship with him.

Richard Rohr, *Falling Upward* (London: SPCK, 2012)
I'm including this book because I have found it to be particularly motivating as I progress through my 'second half of life'.

Feedback
I'm always interested to receive feedback, especially on your encounters with Jesus, however they turn out. I'd like to hear about that and whether you found this material helpful or difficult. If you would like to contact me, please do so using this email address: **acsmith7000@gmail.com**

For more information visit: **www.ionacrossing.com**